Imagined Families,
Lived Families

Imagined Families, Lived Families

Culture and Kinship in Contemporary Japan

Edited by

Akiko Hashimoto

and

John W. Traphagan

Published by State University of New York Press, Albany

Printed in the United States of America

For information, contact State University of New York Press, Albany, NY
www.sunypress.edu

Production by Kelli W. LeRoux
Marketing by Michael Campochiaro

Library of Congress Cataloging-in-Publication Data

Imagined families, lived families : culture and kinship in contemporary
    Japan / edited by Akiko Hashimoto and John W. Traphagan.
        p. cm.
    Includes bibliographical references and index.
    ISBN 978-0-7914-7577-5 (hardcover : alk. paper)
    ISBN 978-0-7914-7578-2 (softcover : alk. paper)
    1. Family—Japan.   I. Hashimoto, Akiko, 1952–   II. Traphagan, John W.

HQ682.I43 2008
306.850952—dc22   2008003134

10 9 8 7 6 5 4 3 2 1

This book is dedicated to L. Keith Brown, who has been a friend and mentor to the editors and many others who have been fortunate to know and work with him over the years.

We also wish to dedicate this book to the memory of Keiko McDonald, who passed away suddenly shortly before publication. All of us will miss her greatly.

Contents

Illustrations

Acknowledgments

This book emerged from a symposium on the family in Japan held at the University of Pittsburgh in the fall of 2004. In addition to the participants who presented papers, several scholars participated as discussants. We would like to thank each—Merry White, Hiroshi Nara, Keith Brown, and Paul Noguchi—for their contributions to the ideas that have emerged in this volume. The editors would also like to acknowledge the help of a variety of people and organizations who contributed greatly to the production of this volume. Funding to support this project was provided by a variety of organizations. At the University of Pittsburgh generous support was received from the Japan Iron and Steel Federation/Mitsubishi Endowments, the Asian Studies Center, the University Center for International Studies, and the School of Arts and Sciences. We also thankfully acknowledge support from the Toshiba International Foundation. At the University of Texas at Austin, support was provided by the Center for East Asian Studies and the Department of Asian Studies. We are also grateful for support from the Mitsubishi Heavy Industries Endowment in Japanese Studies at the University of Texas at Austin. We would also like to thank staff from the Asian Studies Center at the University of Pittsburgh and the Center for East Asian Studies at the University of Texas at Austin for administrative support. Finally, we greatly appreciate the ongoing support of the Japan Council and Hiroyuki Nagahashi Good at the University of Pittsburgh and the work of Linda Takamine from the University of Texas at Austin in preparing the final version of the manuscript. Many thanks also go to Maeri Megumi of the University of Texas at Austin for her work in preparing the index and proofing romanization.

We are grateful to Mitsuhashi Chikako for use of her cartoon from the collected strips in the book *Hāi Ak'ko desu (Hi, I'm Ak'ko) 1*. (Tokyo: Asahi Shinbunsha, 1996), pp. 42–43, and to Ishii Hisaichi and Sōgensha for use of his cartoon *Tonari no Yamada-kun (My Neighbors Yamada)*.

Chapter 1

Changing Japanese Families

Akiko Hashimoto and John W. Traphagan

Introduction

In today's shifting demographic landscape, Japan faces a population dynamic altered greatly from a generation ago. The steady decline in the birth rate has reduced the size of the child population, and at the same time, the continual rise in life expectancy has created a burgeoning pool of elderly people. The cumulative effect of these trends is that the total number of Japanese over age sixty-five now exceeds that of children under age fourteen for the first time.[1] As Japan faces this new demographic topography at the social crossroads of the postindustrial age, the Japanese family in transition is beginning to attract renewed attention of many observers of Japan concerned with the cultural and social consequences of late modernity. This attention also comes at an important time when the results of recent scholarship by feminist sociologists and historians in Japan have cast a new light on the Japanese family. This book addresses the Japanese family—as at once lived experience and imagined social and cultural construct—amid these continually changing social conditions.

At the beginning of the twenty-first century, Japan has entered a period of accelerated social change,[2] following the economic downturn and the restructuring of the "postwar" social system. This has created a context in which people have been forced to confront and reconsider past categories and assumptions about life, family, school, and workplace. In many ways, past categories and assumptions seem out of sync with today's social and economic demands. In this environment of discontinuity, reimagining the family and individual family roles and relationships within the family becomes an important element of a social discourse that shapes the experience of family life. As Anthony Giddens (1992) has observed, the transformation of intimacy is inevitable when past institutional arrangements lose their hold on contemporary life.

1

Opting out of prototypical "traditional" family arrangements seems increasingly feasible when the global media not only broadens our awareness of different family lifestyles, but also economic uncertainties have undermined past expectations. In Japan today, this "opting out" is expressed especially in the decreasing significance of marriage and child rearing among successive younger generations (White 2002). Millions of young Japanese adults today opt to delay marriage until later in life than in the past, and particularly for women, decide to forego marriage completely. Indeed, Ministry of Health Labor and Welfare statistics show that the mean age of marriage has increased from 25.9 for men and 23.0 for women in 1950 to 29.6 and 27.8 respectively in 2004.[3] Sex and marriage have often been de-linked, and thus, premarital sex is the norm in contemporary Japanese society (Nakanishi 2004). It is therefore not surprising that a large proportion of young adults now endorse the idea of couples living together without marriage registration (Mainichi Shinbun 2004). Experimentation in alternative family arrangements has recently become sufficiently interesting to the general public that a popular magazine ran a feature story on couples who pursue what is known as "neo-marriage" (*neo-kekkon*) where friends are added to the family as housemates (AERA 2005). Whether this represents a new trend, or a new version of a historical pattern in extended families to define members of a household in fairly broad terms, as has L. K. Brown argued, is as yet not clear (Brown 1966, 1131). In either case, evidence suggests that the rising desire and need to revise the "prototypical" family in the past decades has been clearly influenced by the increase in women's gainful employment and economic self-sufficiency (Ochiai 1989).

The declining aspirations for child rearing also point to some changes in the expectations for parent-child relations (Yamada 2001; Nakanishi 2004). Today's youths, when asked about their ideal image of parents, overwhelmingly say that they want their parents to be "like friends" (*tomodachi no yōna oya*) (White 1993). This contrasts against images of traditional parenting still found among older generations in rural regions where, as one of John W. Traphagan's informants put it, "children are [viewed as] the belongings of their parents. They are the parents' pets" (*shoyū dōbutsu*)"[4] (Traphagan 2000, 377). These sentiments surely attest to the children's desire for nonauthoritarian parenting, a finding consistent with most other youth surveys. Yet, this desire to have the parents act like their peers also points to an unarticulated ideal about parenting, with a somewhat indeterminate view of what specifically the parents can do for the children (Hashimoto 2004a). At the same time, recent surveys have also shown that, given the choice between one's own happiness and that of the family, a sizeable proportion of young people today would privilege their own happiness and eschew family sacrifices[5]—although how this actually plays out when a family crisis arises is difficult to determine (Traphagan 2002).

Feminist sociologist Meguro Yoriko (1987) has claimed that these changes amount to the coming of "individualized" families in Japan, a trend toward a redefinition of relationships between individuals and collectivities. This trend is akin to what some American sociologists call the "coming of postmodern families"—diverse families that come together as voluntary social units that privilege individual needs over "traditional" institutionalized arrangements (Stacey 1996; Castells 1997).[6] In American society today, a wide variety of families—single-parent families, blended families, stepfamilies, cohabitating couples, childless couples, gay and lesbian families, and other variations—replace the prototypical nuclear family, and comprise the majority of families. By comparison, the changes that have reconfigured the family terrain in the recent decade in Japan are increasing singlehood, late marriages, divorce, domestic violence and elder abuse. Individualization of or in the family, however, does not necessarily mean that Japanese society is hospitable to individuals living independently, nor does it imply that Japan is following a path of individuation that parallels or mirrors exactly that followed in the United States or other industrial countries.

The Family and Social Change

The Japanese family, like family elsewhere, has historically been varied and mutable. Over the centuries, it has seen much regional and class variation in patterns of marriage, succession, and levels of sexual freedom. From the less regulated and more egalitarian pairing families before the formal social organization of the eighth century through the emergence of the patriarchal family, control over family succession and inheritance mattered mostly for the elite class. Patriarchy, first established among the aristocracy, gained strength under the military rule in feudal Japan when marriages were serious political business for the elites. Thus developed the *ie*, a type of stem family system for the elite—particularly in the Edo (1603–1867) and Meiji (1868–1912) periods—which is now commonly referred to as *the* traditional Japanese family. The stem family of the Edo period, as part of a patriarchal order, embodied social hierarchy and the assumption of men's privilege over women. With it, the elite woman's ability to own assets, and maintain her surname after marriage also became less and less tenable (Sekiguchi et al. 2000).

When Japan encountered modernity in the end of the nineteenth century, Japanese leaders found themselves faced with a difficult issue of forging a nation-state among people who had been inhabitants of disparate feudal domains. The solution to the problem was to reimagine the family by legally extending the *ie* family system that had been common among the elite to the entire population, and thereby enforce a national regulation of family life. The Family Law in 1898 formally established a stem family system that stipulated primogeniture, the passage of family headship succession and allocation of rights of inheritance of the entire estate from eldest son to eldest son. Thus, the Meiji state established the central regulation of the family, and arranged marriages spread thereafter in the late nineteenth century. The state also enforced laws to make married couples use the same surname, and intensified the domestication of women, and the sexual division of labor (Sekiguchi et al. 2000, 8). This regime therefore empowered the male head of households, and disempowered female family members by prohibiting them from making decisions about property, assets, marriage, or divorce. Women thereby lost legal rights as autonomous social agents. At the same time, patriarchal ideology also took on a national dimension with the stipulation of the notion that the emperor was the supreme patriarch of the nation. For the purpose of mobilization, taxation, and control, an intense ideological campaign sought to situate loyalty to the state above the family, and promoted the notion that the state was itself the ultimate big "family," with the emperor's family as the main family from which all others are offshoots.

Of course, the fact that the family was formally reconceptualized legally, in terms of primogeniture and a strict division of rights and obligations on the basis of gender and birth order, does not mean that family life was necessarily *experienced* along these lines. While many, perhaps most, families became organized around the *ie* structure, the mere facts of biology necessitate variation and inventiveness—families may lack sons, lack children, or prior traditions may stipulate the importance of matriarchal inheritance as M. Yoshida points out (1997). The heavy disruption and losses wrought by the fifteen year war in the Asia-Pacific also diminished the continuity of this system for many families (Sekiguchi et al. 2000).

In the wake of World War II, Japanese people experienced another formal revision of the family system as the patriarchal stem family and primogeniture were formally abolished due to political and social restructuring and planning dictated by the American Occupation. Since then the Japanese family has experienced a series of major reconceptualizations. The Family Law of 1947, enacted during the American Occupation, had considerable social consequences. To use the common refrain, as Japan ushered in the new postwar era, the Japanese family discarded its old garb—the *ie* and primogeniture systems—and effectively remade itself in a new image modeled largely on the "Western" democratic ideal of the nuclear family. This was a radical makeover: the "new" postwar family was represented in the language of equality, individual rights, freedom of choice, and voluntary unions—civic principles derived from a Euro-American paradigm that was entirely distinct from the preceding Confucian patriarchy. The prewar authoritarian way of life, the "feudal" (*hōkenteki*) way of life, was now seemingly cast aside, discredited, and consigned to history (Smith 1996). The new family promised to turn a new leaf, and promote family relations based on democratic and individualistic rules of engagement (Kawashima 1950; Hashimoto 2004a). Based on the fundamental legal changes and economic expansion of the postwar era, family practices were transformed in patterns of marriage, urban, and suburban residential patterns, and the life course (Hashimoto 2004b). Yet at the same time, even with the internal momentum to reconstitute the family, basic structures associated with the *ie*, such as an emphasis on birth order in terms of identifying which child is likely to have primary responsibility to care for parents, continued to influence conceptualizations about roles, rights, and responsibilities especially within rural families (Traphagan 2000, 2004a, 2004b).

Changing Aspirations for Family Life (1940s–1970s)

Given this recent history, it is not surprising that both premodern and postmodern elements coexist in contemporary Japanese families. Japanese people today create, especially in the realm of aspirations and desires, a hybrid model of family. This is because Japan's transformation in the second half of the twentieth century was not a simple transition from *ie* to the nuclear family, but a product of myriad economic and social compromises between the focus on male lineage and mother-daughter-in-law struggles on the one hand, and aspirations for a loving home and a private space for parents to raise their children without interference, on the other hand. The influence of the Eurocentric modern family that idealized family love had already arrived in Japan by the early 1900s. Thus, the ideals of romantic conjugal love and the strong mother-child bond became part of the intellectual discourse, if not necessarily a widespread practice, at that time. The entrance of this ideal of romantic conjugal love was connected to processes of imagining and reimagining the family as it entered the youthful consciousness through media and entertainment even as the large proportion of mate selection remained under control of the parents. The strength of mother-child love, commonly believed to be a "traditional" legacy from prewar Japan is in fact also greatly influenced by European and American literature, films, and intellectual discourse

(Sakamoto 1997, 34, 153). In the course of such modern transformation, the bonds with extended kin became more peripheral, while the bonds among nuclear family members grew more intense and emotional (Yamada 2001). At the same time, while continuities from the past such as patriarchical hierarchies became less visible in the foreground, it nevertheless remained a salient part of family life especially in rural Japan.

Changes in Romantic Love and Marriage

The degree to which romantic love has come to dominate the ideals of intimacy and privacy for the couple in the imaginations of Japanese—emphasizing love, emotional bonds, personal attraction, compatibility, and individual choice for marriage—has been remarkable. Romantic love marriage overtook arranged marriage around 1970 as the popular form of marital choice; today they comprise almost all marriages (figure 1.1).[7] Such marriages also began to shift later in age as the notion of individual choice became more desirable. While almost all women (95%) in their early thirties were married in 1950, fifty years later, the proportion had declined by almost one third, to 66 percent (Sekiguchi et al., 2000, 187). Today, only 18 percent of young people aged 18–24 feel that everyone should marry (Yuzawa 2003, 103). This perspective derives partly from the ideology of romantic love, and at the same time, it may also reflect their sense that the prospect of living with in-laws is unattractive (Yuzawa 2003, 97). The hybrid model of marriage is evident in the fact that despite the trend toward autonomy, couples still find it necessary to ponder whether or not to live with the in-laws. J. M. Raymo (2003b) has argued that delayed marriage or a decision not to marry at all is associated with high levels of educational attainment and suggests that this may be connected to the social milieu of Japan in which it is difficult for women to balance work and family.

Another consequence of the changing marriage practices has been the declining birth rate. Japan's total fertility rate dropped below the replacement rate of 2.1 in 1974 and has hovered around 1.3 children per woman over the life course since 1997, reaching 1.29 in 2003.[8] It seems likely that delayed marriage or refusal to marry has contributed to the low total fertility rate in recent years, as a growing number of women are choosing not to have children. In the meantime, Japanese marriages have diversified further: the proportion of those who had experienced cohabitation without marriage reached 15 percent of women aged 20–49 in a recent survey (Mainichi Shinbun 2004); paper divorce is a practice now found among those who oppose the law that legal marriage requires couples to adopt the same surname; in-house divorce is another trend

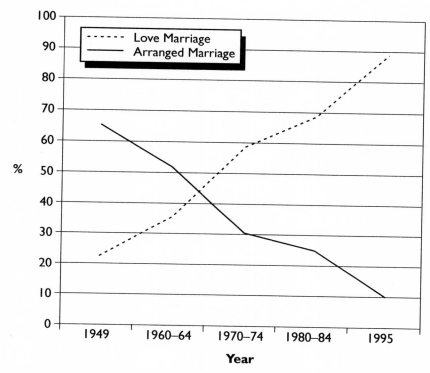

Source: Japan Ministry of Health and Welfare, 11th Shussei dōkō kihon chōsa 1998 (cited in Yuzawa 2003), 93.

Figure 1.1 Changes in Proportions of Love Marriages and Arranged Marriages, 1949–1995

known among estranged couples who continue their legal marriage while divorced emotionally.[9]

Changes in Maternal Love and Domesticity

As historical sociologist Ochiai Emiko (1989, 237) has documented, modernity is also a time when the regard for the woman as a mother and the infant as a person heightened in the family. By the second half of the twentieth century, the figure responsible for the well-being of life at home shifted quite noticeably from the father figure to the mother figure. Indeed the loss of the powerful father figure is a recurrent theme in discussions of the postwar Japanese family, as the war had destabilized masculine identity and along with it, his authority in the family (Yamada 2001, 356). This loss of a dignified male presence invariably forced a deepening reliance on the mother figure as the solid and dependable anchor of the family, a figure that had emerged untarnished by the violence, failure, and culpability in the war (Saitō 2003). The ideal postwar mother is also the solidly dependable figure who is always there to offer love and nurturance, in contrast to the ideal prewar mother who is predominantly imagined as the self-sacrificing, suffering figure (Sakamoto 1997, 176). Such myth of maternal love and maternal society intensified further in the enterprise society of the 1960s (Yoda 2000, 866).

Moreover, the powerful aspirations for the "new family" came in the context of the emerging economic affluence of Japanese society and spurred by the consumer revolution and the economic expansion in the 1960s and 1970s. The "new family" was Japan's new middle class, typically in suburban homes equipped with consumer gadgets that ostensibly made the life of the housewife comfortable. This is the "salaryman" family that Ezra Vogel discusses in his work on the Japanese family in the 1960s; the nuclear family organized around the bureaucracies and businesses of postwar Japan that constituted a male domain juxtaposed against the female domain of the domestic sphere. The new family was the postwar version of the modern family, founded on reintensified gender division of labor. This new domesticity was also centered on the mother, who took almost the entire responsibility for child rearing and hearth tending (Yoda 2000).

The new family ideal was based on an ideology of home ownership called "my home-ism" in which urban middle-class workers aspired to a matricentric image of domesticity (Yoda 2000, 871). In a sense, postwar affluence and consumer culture greatly influenced and also depended on women's domestic aspirations and choices (Miura 1999). Unlike their mothers who had assumed more passive roles in the prewar family, postwar mothers were expected to be the creators of comfort at home, nurturing their family with love, care, and nourishing food. Since there were limited role models for this in urban Japan, fictive models from American sitcoms, Japanese home dramas on television, weekly women's magazines, and the flood of advertising became influential. The new family was supposed to be bright, sweet, and happy, like those fictive models. Mass aspiration for the middle-class new family was to erase class disparity, and realize the Japanese dream. Additionally, the idealization of home tended by the full time housewife that served as a refuge from the working world for men also helped to legitimate the excessive workload of that world. By 1975, the proportion of women who were housewives overseeing the domestic domain reached its highest peak

(Miura 1999). At around the same time, the growth of nuclear families also plateaued. Thereafter, co-residence with the elderly began to decline at the rate of 1 percent per year (Hashimoto and Ikels 2005). By the 1980s, however, the weight of contradictions between the dream and the reality of domesticity, finally began to expose.

The Transformation of Intimacy (1980s–2000s)

Anthony Giddens (1992) has pointed out that the transformation of intimacy occurs when relationships are freed from the confines and regulations of institutional arrangements at particular historical moments. At these junctures, the dissonance and contradiction between chosen bonds and institutional bonds become inescapable and create uncertainty. This is the case also for Japan in the 1990s and 2000s, especially in regard to parent-child relationships (Yamada 2001, 186).

By the 1980s, when Japan had achieved the prosperity it aspired to in the early postwar period, the children raised in the new families of suburbia knew already that the happiness that was promised with the idealized "my home-ism" did not resonate with their reality. In many respects, the ideal new families had been made possible by the consumerism that accompanied economic expansion; but when the economic bubble burst and the recession exposed the illusion of permanent and stable employment for the diligent work force, the children found that attaining a better living than their parents through hard work and better education was no longer guaranteed (Yamada 2001, 186). Once parents could no longer guarantee to their children that filial obedience would lead to success, the children's expectations regarding filial bonds shifted to more individualized, voluntary ties. This trend illustrates Yamada Masahiro's thesis that upward mobility can no longer serve as a family or individual goal, and institutional rules and norms geared to its attainment lose their power (2001, 49, 110).[10]

Japanese Families in a Global Age

The preceding discussion provides the context for the chapters that follow in this book. A multidisciplinary group of scholars address Japanese families from a variety of perspectives, including anthropology, political science, sociology, and literature. The key theme that runs through the contributions is an emphasis on how attitudes towards and ideas about the family have changed recently and how the Japanese are in the process, again, of reconsidering or reimagining the nature of the family. The contributors look at conceptualizations of family expressed within families, particularly those faced with traumatic issues such as abandonment or long-term illness, as well as the public imagination about the family through media such as *anime* and *manga*.

Our primary interest is in understanding "the family" as a dynamic and continually changing social unit that does not simply exist, but is imagined or conceptualized and reconceptualized in the minds of individual people and in public discourse. A. Hashimoto's chapter 2, S. Napier's chapter 3, and K. McDonald's chapter 4 examine representations of family in the popular media, such as newspaper comics (*manga*), animation (*anime*), and films. Hashimoto explores changes in the power dynamics among family members represented in comics over the last half century. Each successive generation reinterprets and redefines the notion of the "good" family as the times change, and they often reflect the tensions and conflicts of competing ideals. Napier argues that science fiction and fantasy texts found in animated films showcase discourses on the family precisely because the genres defamiliarize common issues such as intergenerational conflict, sibling rivalry, and even geriatric problems. She looks at popular films such as *Spirited Away* to show how alternative visions of family are portrayed and represented in popular culture. Turning to family issues that arise in relation to the end of life, McDonald considers the work of two female Japanese film directors and the images of aging and senile dementia that they portray. These films, endorsed by the Ministry of Education, represent the state-sanctioned perspectives and ideologies on the family, which are also constructed by women.

From these studies of fiction, the volume turns to a variety of social and political issues that have affected the Japanese family over the past sixty years. Steinhoff examines the families of political dissidents who were prominent members of the protest movements of the 1960s, and explores the family crises that ensued as a direct result of political activism, arrests, and state prosecution. Tamanoi takes a historical perspective and examines the problem of returnees from Manchuria, once abandoned in 1945, now seeking reunion with their Japanese families of origin. She expands the scope of her inquiry to the friction between "the Japanese" who emigrated to Northeast China (Manchuria) in the 1930s and were subsequently repatriated with their "Chinese" families, and "the Japanese" who never left mainland Japan, to challenge the perception that Japan is "a big family." Long raises important questions about recent changes in family configurations and the effects on caregiving for the elderly. She shows concomitant strains of aligning roles and responsibilities, in difficult family circumstances filled with a sense of loss.

In summary, the chapters in this volume represent "the family" in Japan as a dynamic and changing unit that is interpreted in a variety of ways. As several Japan scholars have shown in recent years (cf. Goodman 2002; Traphagan 2003), no single representation of the family is adequate for understanding the manner in which families function and are understood in the Japanese context. What emerges from these chapters is a picture of complex Japanese families in which a variety of traditional and modern ideas and hybrid ideologies influence decision making within families and attitudes about what constitutes a family in the modern Japanese context. The family is not a stagnate entity, but is continually changing as individuals experience familial relationships within the framework of both the immediate social milieu and, increasingly in the twenty-first century, in a context of global informational exchange that exposes people to a variety of possibilities around which to imagine their own life situation.

Notes

Changing Japanese Families

1. Demographic conditions of family relations are projected to change further during this century. At the current replacement rate, the population of Japan will shrink from the current 127 million to approximately 64 million by the end of the twenty-first century. Those over the age of sixty-five are expected to increase from just under 20 percent of the population in 2005 to a peak of almost 36 percent in 2055 and will remain over 35 percent for the rest of the century. By contrast, those between the ages of zero and fourteen will drop from slightly under 14 percent of the population in 2005 to a low of about 10.5 percent in 2055 (See Traphagan and Knight 2003).

2. We refer here to a speed of change under recent globalization trends that appears to be faster than in previous decades, measured in terms of significant socioeconomic indicators (Giddens 2000; Held et. al. 1999; Sassen 1999).

3. Source: Ministry of Internal Affairs and Communications, Statistical Bureau, http://www.stat.go.jp

4. The Japanese word *shoyū dōbutsu* 所有動物 literally means "owned animal."

5. This is especially the case for women. Nihon Seishōnen Kenkyūjo. 2004. *Kōkōsei no gakushū ishiki to nichijō seikatsu: Nihon, amerika, chūgoku no 3 kakoku hikaku.* (Tokyo: Nihon Seishōnen Kenkyūjo), p. 87. http://www1.odn. ne.jp/youth-study/reserch/2005/danjo.pdf

6. The prototypical nuclear family consisting of father, mother, and one or two unmarried children now comprise only 25 percent of all American families.

7. The classification of love marriages and arranged marriages usually relies on self-report of respondents in social surveys that do not offer the hybrid form combining the two. Such hybrid forms may be more salient in rural areas than urban cities.

8. Source: Japan Statistical Yearbook online. http://www.stat.go.jp/english/data/nenkan/1431-02.htm. Accessed 9 January 2006.

9. See Masahiro, Yamada. 2001. *Kazoku to iu risuku (The Family Risk)*. (Tokyo: Keisō Shobō).

10. Yamada argues that parent-child attachments have been rather materialistic and instrumental. Thus, he suggests that parent-child relations have been sustained mainly by need satisfaction, especially in the high economic growth and bubble periods (1960s, 1970s and 1980s).

Imagined Families

Chapter 2

Blondie, Sazae, and Their Storied Successors

Japanese Families in Newspaper Comics

Akiko Hashimoto

The twentieth century was one of the most turbulent periods of Japanese history. In the first half of the century, Japan moved from imperial expansion into totalitarianism and violent global wars. In the second half of the century, following defeat in World War II, Japan undertook a massive transformation of socioeconomic and political systems that led to unprecedented economic growth. The Japanese population responded to the pressures of such dramatic changes by adapting their cultural ideologies to new social realities, sometimes bending with the wind, other times standing against the wind, but either way, with significant and enduring changes in their personal lives.

This chapter explores the cultural dynamics of these changes in Japan, focusing on the Japanese family especially over the postwar years. It traces the shifting discourses of the family that each successive generation defined in its own terms, as they were contested and accommodated throughout the last six decades. It charts these discourses through representations of popular characters in the Japanese cultural media, devoting special attention to five popular fictive families in well-known newspaper comics that reached millions of households between 1949 and 2006. As the family continually both adjusts to and resists the changing social environment, it becomes not only a place where stable personal relations develop, but also a site where divergent family ideologies collide (Shapiro 2001).

The Japanese Family in Modernity

Japanese sociologists examining family and gender, such as Ueno Chizuko and Ochiai Emiko, have recently articulated valuable perspectives on the history of the Japanese family (Ueno 1994; Ochiai 1989; Meguro, 1987; Sakai 1995). They have shown, for example, that the "modern family" was largely a product of the twentieth century, common in both prewar *and* postwar Japan (Sekiguchi et al. 2000). They also showed that there is much continuity from the prewar through the postwar periods in patriarchal relations and emotional dynamics, between parents and children, husband and wife, and also among siblings—despite the legal changes of 1947 (Ueno 1994, 80). Rather than a simple transition from the traditional stem family in prewar society to the modern family in postwar society that many have claimed, Japan's experience in the twentieth century was an ongoing reconfiguration that wove together premodern, modern, and postmodern elements, creating a synthetic family model throughout. The changing experience of the family was therefore neither a linear transition from the old to the new, nor a complete replacement of the old by the new, but a complex combination of both.

These insights fly in the face of popular beliefs concerning "the demise of the traditional family of the golden days": the nostalgic thesis that modernity has somehow wrought a terrible destruction in the values of the traditional extended family, to replace them with those of the isolated nuclear family. But we have learned that the nuclear family was in fact already a mainstay in early twentieth-century Japan, and remained prevalent for the whole century (table 2.1).[1] Moreover, this pattern probably existed even in the nineteenth century, when the average household size was about five persons (Ochiai 1994, 200). In other words, the nuclear family has been a common family type in Japan for much longer than popular beliefs would have us assume. The *proportion* of the extended family has declined because of increasing single households, not because of mushrooming nuclear households. Actually, the average number of children that Japanese couples have had in the past decades has been virtually the same (Yamada 2001, 210).[2]

The gap between popular beliefs in the extended family and the prevailing reality of the nuclear family presents us with interesting clues

Table 2.1   Family Trends in Japan, 1920–2000

	1920 %	1955 %	1965 %	1975 %	1985 %	1995 %	2000 %
Nuclear	54	61	63	64	60	59	59
Extended	39	36	30	22	19	16	14
Single	7	3	8	14	21	26	27

Source: Yuzawa (Tokyo: NHK Books, 2003), 19.

about how we construct and perpetuate nostalgic ideals. There are many factors at work, from media messages to state policy and elite ideology. First, the "traditional" extended family has been portrayed as the prototype of the ideal family by the popular media through most of the postwar years. The image of the happy multigenerational family as an ideal model dominated the popular media and appeared in many forms in television and films appealing to a wide range of viewers. Sometimes the images were nostalgic portraits of real or invented families of a bygone era; others projected amiable families that people could aspire to; and still others promoted "happiness" that fitted into the business agenda of the entertainment industry (Higuchi 2002, 147–48; Ivy 1995). Images of harmonious extended families attracted successive generations, in television, films, magazines, books, and other entertainment media (Goessmann 2000). The ideal images of togetherness in multigenerational families were commonplace in the newspaper comic, and attracted a broad audience throughout the postwar years (Hashimoto and Traphagan 2004).

Second, the Japanese state has routinely promoted social policies—like welfare and labor policies—that presupposed the traditional family. As in most nation-states past and present, Japan always had a vested interest in controlling citizens' family life to monitor fertility, labor, and national duties. At the end of the nineteenth century, the Meiji state required people to mold their family life to fit primogeniture of the stem family system ie, which conveniently served the purposes of disciplining labor, taxation, and military conscription. Then, in the wake of World War II at the end of the 1940s, acting through the Japanese state, the U.S. Occupation required citizens to reinvent their family lives again to fit a new family ideology: the democratic nuclear family. This time, the "feudalistic" family was transformed into a supposedly better transnational model, based on civic principles of equality, rights, and freedom of choice. But by the 1970s, the state again asked its people, especially women, to reinvigorate their sense of familial duty in an effort to support the state's aging and welfare policies. More recently, the state has continued to pursue this line of persuasion in its fertility policies, sounding the alarm again about the breakdown of "family values," in an attempt to entice women to have more children (White 2002, 3).

Third, Japan's intellectual elites have often emphasized the ideal of the traditional stem family (ie) as a central metaphor for national identity, and have used the metaphor of an imaginary family for the Japanese nation to foster the sense of unity and counter the sense of threat from the international world (Aoki 1990; Harootunian 1989). In prewar militarist Japan, the crucial ideology for strengthening national solidarity was the notion that Japanese citizens were, by the simple fact of being Japanese, all children of the emperor. After military defeat, this homogenizing ideology had to be abandoned, but it did not entirely fade from national consciousness. In the 1960s and 1970s, the family metaphor reemerged in a different guise in the national discourse on Japaneseness (*Nihonjinron*) and often served as a key ideology that promoted workers' attachment and loyalty to their employers (Murakami et al., 1979; Nakane 1967).

Nostalgia for the imagined "traditional" family is certainly a phenomenon common in societies experiencing rapid change, and it is surely not unique to Japan (Hareven 1978; Laslett 1972). Some of the nostalgia for the imagined past no doubt reflects a social anxiety over the shifting power dynamics between men and women, and the old and young. In postwar Japan, the democratic family was meant to privilege the concerns for individual rights and equality rather than status obligations, lineage or succession (Ueno 1994; Ochiai 1989). Against this backdrop, the ideals of romantic love and gender equality steadily pushed aside arranged marriages, so that romantic love marriages began to dominate mate selection by the 1970s, when the baby boomers came of age. Yet, even as the romantic love match seemed to promote greater individual freedom, it did not escape being an object of regulation in modern society, as it meant that now everyone *had to* marry as soon as he/she fell in love (Yamada 2001, 182–83). In intergenerational relations, including relationships between parent and child, the modified expectations are such that today's children, when asked about their ideal image of parents, overwhelmingly say that they want their parents to be "like friends" (*tomodachi no yōna oya*). These sentiments expressed by Japanese children surely attest to their desire for nonauthoritarian parenting, a finding consistent with most other youth surveys (White 1993). Yet, this desire to have parents act like peers also points to an unrealistic expectation of parenting, a vague understanding of what specifically the parents can do for the children, and vice versa.

Family Comics in Japanese Newspapers

Modern newspaper comics reach millions of readers in all corners of the world as cultural products of mass entertainment, employing an identical format and dissemination technique. They first reached Japan in the 1900s, introduced by the artist Kitazawa Rakuten who was inspired by early American comic strips (Shimizu 1991). Because Japan already had its own flourishing visual arts of satire and humor at the time, it did not take long for them to become successful commodities of mass consumption. The popularity of such newspaper cartoons soared especially in the second half of the twentieth century, when they grew rapidly into diverse commercial products like *manga* books, television anime series, anime films, thousands of paraphernalia, theme parks, and museums (Kinsella 2000, Duus 1988).

Mass circulation newspaper comic strips appeal widely to readers in Japan as elsewhere especially when they succeed in poignantly exposing the contradictions and anxieties of the times. They accomplish this by revealing hidden or unexpected assumptions underlying social routines and expectations, often to hilarious effect. Just as Garfinkel's ethnomethodological experiments effectively disrupted everyday encounters to reveal much of what we take for granted, daily comics can also expose the absurdities of familiar expectations and formalities. They therefore reach beyond the superficial surface of life, shake readers out of complacency, and touch an emotional chord without being threatening. Some of the funniest comics can pierce through appearances, and allow readers to reach a deeper self-understanding while letting their hair down, putting their feet up, and sharing a laugh. Along the way, they can offer a safety zone, a comic relief of the day, and a space for thumbing one's nose at authority figures—by caricaturing parents, teachers, police officers, politicians, and prime ministers. As the cartoonists spin their tales, readers confront their own conformity and resistance to the nuisance called "social order."

The five popular families appearing here have all been serialized in the national newspaper *Asahi Shinbun* which has a broad circulation of over eight million. They are not portrayed to be representative Japanese families, but rather are popular Japanese families in the imaginary world of fiction that have consistently won the affection of loyal readers over the last six decades. These fictitious families—*Blondie*, *Sazae-san* (and its spin-off *Granny Mischief* in *Sunday Mainichi*), *Hi, I'm Ak'ko*, *My Neighbors Yamada* (later renamed *Nono-chan*), and *People of the Earth Defense Family* (table 2.2)—continue to capture the public imagination today, beyond the original *Asahi* readership of decades ago.[3]

Table 2.2   Five Family Comics in the Asahi Newspaper, 1949–present

1949–1951	*Blondie*
1951–1974	*Sazae-san* (and its spin-off *Granny Mischief*)
1980–2002	*Hi, I'm Ak'ko*
1991–	*My Neighbors Yamada* (later renamed *Nono-chan*)
2002–	*People of the Earth Defense Family*

Source: Shinbun Manga Kenkyūjo, "Shinbun keisai no manga ichiran." In *Shinbun Manga Kenkyūjo* 2002, vol. 8. http://www5d.biglobe.ne.jp/~shinbun/index.html. Accessed 7/13/2003.

With the exception of *Blondie*, these comics remain in print today as paperbacks, and have also been popularized in television series, anime series, or commercial films. *Sazae-san*, which ran in the *Asahi* newspaper for twenty-five years, has been published in volumes that have sold over 80 million copies to date. Likewise, *Hi, I'm Ak'ko* ran in the *Asahi* for twenty-two years and continues to sell well in paperback volumes. *Sazae, Granny, Ak'ko* and *My Neighbors* were all made into well-known television weeklies and some became profitable commercial films as well. All in all, these comics as mass media commodities have succeeded enormously in invoking the popular fantasies and desires of readers and audiences across generations.

Blondie, 1949–1951

During the American Occupation, Chic Young's classic *Blondie* was one of the first comic strips to be serialized in Japanese newspapers. The series was published in the daily *Asahi* newspaper 1949 to 1951, and also in the weekly *Asahi* from 1946 to 1956 (Iwamoto 1997, 155). *Blondie*'s illustrious middle-class lifestyle depicted in Japanese translation held an immense appeal for readers in a way that may surprise us today. Old-time readers who reminisce about it speak of being stunned by the affluence of the apparently ordinary couple who owned a house, a car, an electric washing machine, a well-stocked refrigerator, and even a family dog (Iwamoto 1998). As such, *Blondie* planted the seed of the American Dream in the neocolonial state of occupied Japan, and helped inspire "the popular envy of the consumerism and material comforts of American-style 'democracy' " (Dower 1999, 252). The enchantment with *Blondie*'s lifestyle and material comforts therefore ignited a powerful desire in the readers for Americanization that also came to be dubbed *coca-colonization* in Europe around the same time (Wagnleitner 1994).

Meanwhile, the appeal of Blondie and Dagwood's romantic relationship as an ideal model of marriage for the readers of the time is more difficult to assess. Their passionate and demonstrative romantic love must have certainly presented a stark contrast to Japan's conjugal relations of the time. Furthermore, it is unclear if the Japanese audience appreciated the fact that this passionate marriage came about through a defiance of parental authority. In marrying Blondie, Dagwood had defied his rich parents who had been bitterly opposed to the marriage. Dagwood's action not only caused family strain, but he also was disinherited by his family. He had therefore forsworn the promise of a rich, comfortable life to start a new family with his true love. It is rather ironic that it was this comparatively plain life of forgone riches that seemed affluent beyond envy to the Japanese readers (Iwamoto 1997, 155).

While *Blondie* might not have exactly fit the Japanese milieu of material life and emotional intimacy of the time, it certainly demonstrated the American family style powerfully. Surely, *Asahi's Blondie* presented the "democratic family" more vividly than the home economics textbooks distributed at the time to schoolchildren by the Ministry of Education and sanctioned by the U.S. Occupation (Sakai 1995). Even if *Blondie's* style of passionate and romantic conjugal love was emotionally "untranslatable" to the Japanese audience at a time when arranged marriages were the norm, it certainly planted the idea that one could and should desire it. When *Blondie* was transplanted to Japan, the national press was still under the control of U.S. military censors, and criticism of the United States and the Allies was suppressed; thus, the Japanese conversion to democratic families began under particularly extreme conditions of persuasion.

Sazae-san, 1951–1974, and its offshoot Granny Mischief, 1966–72

Following *Blondie*, the *Asahi* newspaper published the comic series *Sazae-san* which became arguably the most successful family cartoon series in Japanese history (Hasegawa 1997, 2001). Created by Hasegawa Machiko, a brilliant woman with a phenomenal sense of humor, *Sazae-san* was a four-panel comic strip that depicted the everyday life of the Isono family, an ordinary, multigenerational family of seven well-meaning people in postwar Japan. The star Sazae—the first ever female protagonist in Japanese daily cartoons—was a cheerful, scatterbrained housewife, daughter, and mother in this family, described by Frederik Schodt (1997, 9) as "an ordinary young woman with . . . a big heart and a quirky sense of humor . . . [who coped] with the trials and tribulations of postwar life." She lived in an uxorilocal household with her own parents, not her husband's—a relatively uncommon arrangement at that time which gave her comparative freedom to act unconventionally as a young woman. Everyone in her family had famously entertaining names: Sazae is a kind of shellfish; her husband, Masuo, is named after trout, and her son, Tara, is named after codfish. Sazae's dim younger sister Wakame is named after a seaweed, and her impudent brother, Katsuo, is a bonito fish, and so on (Ishiko 1989). This celebrated family gave readers an inviting setting in which to imagine new kinds of family and community relationships as Japan grew from an occupied defeated country to an affluent consumer society over two and a half decades.

Sazae's extraordinary popularity is not difficult to understand. She represented the common people in her travails of everyday life, irreverent to conventions, social order, and authority. Her travails invariably ended in blunders and mishaps, but always tested the limits of the "new order" in a rapidly changing society. When she defied policemen, reprimanded burglars, and went on joy trips with women friends, readers cheered her on enthusiastically because Sazae was a trailblazer in her own way (Schilling 1997; Shindō 1996). Yet, even when she spoke out for gender equality, she remained a homebound woman whose father and husband worked as breadwinners in office jobs. She was oblivious to authority figures, but also benignly obedient and law-abiding. She was a woman liberated from the traditional daughter-in-law role (*yome*), but ultimately conservative in her expectations about domesticity (Higuchi 2006). She took democratic values to heart, yet exercised them only in her small everyday confines. In the fairy tale world of unrealistic happenings and absurd consequences, Sazae succeeded in exposing the contradictions of the new egalitarian and democratic values within her reach, and did so with the most heartening and reassuring naivety.

Sazae-san was serialized in *Asahi* for twenty-five years, and its heroine became a national icon that everyone loved and identified with. *Sazae-san* is the most well-known family comic series in history, cited even in children's home economics textbooks today. Eighty-six million copies of *Sazae-san* books have been sold to date, long after the author's death. All episodes are still in reprint today in a series of sixty-eight volumes, and English translations are also available. *Sazae-san* also became a popular animation television series, and was converted into nine feature films. It is still considered the best-loved cartoon program of all time (Schodt 1997).

Hasegawa's *Sazae-san* spin-off, called *Granny Mischief*, was first published in the weekly magazine *Sunday Mainichi* in 1966 (Tokyo Sazae-san Gakkai 1993, 203).[4] *Granny Mischief* took an entirely different approach from family comics that showcased the idealized, happy family: it depicted the everyday life of an exceptionally mean and crabby old woman with her family (Tokyo Sazae-san Gakkai 1993). Granny was a cranky, devious mother, mother-in-law, and grandmother in the Ijiwaru family (*ijiwaru* translates as "mean"). Her purpose in life was to make everyone else's life miserable, and she never missed a chance to inflict suffering on her unsuspecting family and neighbors.

No one is spared from her mischief: her sons, daughters-in-law, grandchildren, neighbors, shopkeepers, and even her dead husband. Through her mischief—ruining parties, vacations, and other things— Granny breaks down the stereotype of a benign matron, a maternal figure who nurtures her family. In so doing, Granny reveals the hidden realities and hypocrisies of the "happy extended family."

Granny appeared at a time when social anxieties about aging, care of the elderly, and age-grading were rising in the late 1970s. Media representations like *Granny*, NHK programs like *The Grass Next Door* [Tonarino shibafu], and bestsellers like *Twilight Years* came to mirror those concerns poignantly (Ishiko 1989, 118). By thumbing her nose at state-promoted family values, Granny suggested that not all was rosy and well in the "traditional" family, and that respect for elders was a farce in the changing world (Hashimoto 1997). Granny had everything an elderly woman should want—living with her son, served by her daughter-in-law and surrounded by her grandchildren—yet she was never welcome in the family. She was lonely and superfluous, and had nothing to do all day except to create mischief. She acted as if she was happier than those who had gone to the nursing home, but in reality, she wasn't much better off. So she used her pranks to draw attention to herself. As a classic, six volumes of *Granny Mischief* are still in print today. In 2002, English translations were published in three volumes. *Granny* also became a television series, which was revived several times over the past decades.

Hi, I'm Ak'ko, 1980–2002

Starting in 1980, the *Asahi* Sunday newspaper started the weekly series *Hi, I'm Ak'ko*, which depicted an idealized traditional extended family in which the mother and daughter-in-law got along magnificently (Mitsu-hashi 1984). Focused on this "harmonious" in-law relationship the *Ak'ko* series seemed like a conservative backlash against the turbulent 1970s. Ak'ko was a short, chubby young housewife who was happily married to Jun, a tall and handsome young man she met in school. She cherished her modern love-marriage, but also lived traditionally with his mother Setsuko. In the course of the long series, Ak'ko went from being a naïve newlywed to a mother of two small children, but Setsuko always remained the principled, experienced, and proper lady of the household. Ak'ko's domestic relationship with Setsuko was defined clearly from the outset: Sestuko knew how to run a household, and Ak'ko knew nothing. With Ak'ko in this subordinate position, conflict and defiance were strictly contained, which allowed her romanticized in-law relationship to flourish in the weekly stories. Even as Ak'ko went from being a newlywed to the mother of Tarō and Hanako, she never seemed to age or gain power over her mother-in-law. She remained the cute, young housewife who always made naïve mistakes as she learned to be a proper housewife of the Sakamoto family from the authority. She was always the novice and also lovable for all the mistakes she made; and even when scolded by her mother-in-law, she always managed to get through such episodes with a sparkling smile.

Ak'ko celebrated "family values" by presenting the blissful life in a traditional family. In her domestic space, unruly conflict was almost entirely absent. Any tension with the prim and proper Setsuko, whenever it occurred, was depicted unthreateningly, signaling to the reader that the duo still liked each other, that they remained considerate of each other, and that they both very much wanted the co-residence to work out. Ak'ko never probed alternative living arrangements or questioned the values of remaining a stay-at-home wife, a mother, and a live-in daughter-in-law. As the series evolved, Ak'ko even came to prefer the proper and prim ways of the Sakamotos over the laid-back attitudes of her own parents' family. Jun-chan remained the darling of both Ak'ko and Setsuko, but as he himself evolved over time into an absent husband and son who came home late from work after drinking with his co-workers, the domestic space became almost entirely the women's domain.

This serial about the idealized multigenerational family by Mitsu-hashi Chikako ran in *Asahi*'s Sunday edition for twenty-two years from 1980 to 2002. It is still available in a series of twenty paperbacks, and also became a television animation series for four years. Throughout, *Ak'ko* portrayed how premodern and modern elements of the family mixed and combined in the contemporary family; it celebrated Ak'ko's modern love marriage, yet cleverly deployed it as her key motivation to submit to the traditional ways of the Sakamoto family. It presumed that she would voluntarily transform herself into a "proper" Sakamoto, and do so happily for decidedly modern reasons. The ideals of the old-fashioned relations, once called "feudalistic," became the core of Ak'ko's life, although remodeled in the new language of individual choice.

My Neighbors Yamada, and its Renamed Successor Nono-chan, 1991–present

In the 1990s, while *Ak'ko* was still in print, the *Asahi* newspaper debuted a daily comic series featuring a different kind of family. *My Neighbors Yamada* started in 1991, and it still continues today after being renamed *Nono-chan*.[5] *My Neighbors* is a series of episodic vignettes involving three generations of the Yamada family who live uxorilocally in an unspecified city. The Yamadas are outrageously dim underachievers: the patriarch is a middle-aged salaryman called Takashi who seems to carry no discernable authority. His wife Matsuko is a good-natured but clumsy housewife. Shige is Matsuko's seventy-year-old irritable mother who lives with the Yamada family. Noboru is a teenage son who detests studying, and eight-year-old daughter Non-chan loves only to eat. The family also has a dog Pochi, an ill-humored pet that loathes walks.

In this family, challenges to authority are fair game. The Yamadas are amiable and harmless like their predecessors in *Sazae-san* and *Ak'ko*, but have more egalitarian democratic relationships with one another. They may have conflicts of values and wants, but ultimately resolve them without pulling rank or resorting to family hierarchy. They clash with one another because of individual differences, not because of traditional roles and obligations. The family bond is robust even if the mother cooks poorly, the father makes little money, and the son gets appalling grades. This celebrated democratic family is, not surprisingly, a creation of a baby boomer, Ishii Hisaichi, who is well versed in the postwar discourse of the "new" family.[6] The *Nono-chan* series is still serialized today, and also available in fifteen paperback volumes. It became a television anime series and also a successful animated film in 1999, produced by the czar of Japanese animation Miyazaki Hayato at Studio Ghibli.

The People of the Earth Defense Family, 2002–present

People of the Earth Defense Family is the most recent comic serialized in the *Asahi* evening edition, and started in 2002 (Shiriagari 2004). Created by another baby boomer Shiriagari Kotobuki, this series portrays a nuclear family whose members are timid political activists. Although family cartoons in the *Asahi* newspaper have usually been relatively apolitical, *Earth Defense Family* departs from this trend, and offers more direct social commentary than its predecessors. The mother, father, daughter, and son portrayed in this series are always on the lookout for social evil and corruption. They are always dressed in superhero costumes, ready to mobilize, yet never actually confront anyone. They are heroic in a quixotic way, and passionate about their armchair crusades against social ills, which include everything from environmental pollution and corporate corruption, to political abuse of power.

Unlike their predecessors, members of the Earth Defense Family are nameless and identified only by their family designations: Chichi (father), Haha (mother), Musume (daughter), and Musuko (son). These impersonal designations of individuals, and the title of the series, *hito bito* (people or individuals) of the Earth Defense Family, seem to suggest that these family members are somewhat atomized persons who happen to live together, and that their relationship to each other is more individualistic than their predecessors. Finally, here comes a family whose members relate to one another "like friends," seemingly fulfilling the aspirations for nonauthoritarian parenting that became desirable in postwar families. Sixty years after the ideal of the democratic family entered the Japanese family discourse, contemporary comics like *Earth Defense Family* seem to have shed the vestiges of hierarchical relations that characterized *Sazae-san*, *Granny*, and *Ak'ko*. Yet this fictive family is depicted with surrealism sufficient to deter readers from idealizing or identifying with the individual characters.

Reconfiguring Family Relationships
변형하다.

Scholars of the postwar Japanese family have often observed that a significant turning point in the trend toward "democratization" can be detected in the 1970s, corresponding with the peak of economic growth and the arrival of mass consumer society. It was at this time that baby boomers came of age and started their families in unprecedented numbers; workers in the front lines of economic expansion began to secure their middle-class living in rapidly growing metropolitan suburbs; and full time housewives bound to domesticity reached the highest percentage ever (Miura 1999, 128).

Against this backdrop, an emphasis on women's nurturing role as mothers in the new family began to overshadow the emphasis on serving in-laws (Uno 1993, 304), and the anxieties and struggles of such reconfiguring relationships became visible in popular culture creations like family comics. The mother-in-law was especially a ubiquitous character deployed to explore the tensions of women's changing roles, obligations, and authority. From the 1970s through the 1990s, these characters were invested with strong personalities and varying degrees of authority, ranging from the menacing to the benign. Yet the characterizations of changing family authority relations in newspaper comics were never simple, because they also represented the conservative mission of affirming family values at the same time. The in-law relations illustrated in daily comics tended to promote and legitimate the virtues of family togetherness, even if in reality they were in turmoil. Such illustrations also served to normalize the extended family, even when nuclear families were actually more dominant in Japanese society (Goessmann 2000).

The three mothers-in-law that I explore here are distinct authority figures in the popular fictional families of *Granny Mischief*, *Hi, I'm*

Ak'ko, and *My Neighbors Yamada*. The transition from one character to the next in the course of forty years suggests that the domestic authority of the mother-in-law over younger family members had shifted from the 1970s through the 1990s even in the world of popular culture. In the 1970s, Granny retained considerable control over her daughter-in-law; in the 1980s, however, Setsuko's power over Ak'ko was contingent on Ak'ko's voluntary subservience; by the 1990s, Shige's authority over her son-in-law and daughter had diminished even further.

Typical episodes of *Granny Mischief* in the 1970s often depicted Granny's resistance to yielding authority in the family, especially toward her daughter-in-law Michiko. An episode about housecleaning, for example, showcases Granny's defiance as she puts her considerable harassing skills to use. The episode opens with Granny wiping at an apparent stain on the floor. In fact, the stain is a burn that her daughter-in-law Michiko caused long ago and is therefore permanent. Actually, Granny's motivation in wiping away at it is simply to draw attention to Michiko's mishap, so that she can enjoy Michiko's apology everyday. This is Granny's ploy to keep the upper hand over Michiko. Reflecting the times, this presentation of family relationships suggested that the daughter-in-law had no recourse to resist the authority of the mother-in-law. The daughter-in-law is clearly the subordinate who must defer to Granny, whose authority is uncontested. Yet at the same time, Granny's power is somewhat vacuous, and confined to the most inconsequential details of domestic life. The family knows that the scope of Granny's influence is small, and that fundamentally she is, in old age, a useless dispensable person. She can wreak havoc, but she is superfluous in the family; she can bully the family, but she is ultimately ignored by them. The comedy of Granny's stories comes from the revelations of this family's shameless hypocrisy to one another, while they pretend to live in peaceful harmony.

By contrast, episodes of *Hi, I'm Ak'ko* in the 1980s characterized the mother-in-law's authority over the daughter-in-law as the latter's preference. Here, generational conflict is averted not because of prescribed obedience, but because of chosen strategy. For example, in a vignette that spells out Ak'ko's strategic vision for her relationship with her mother-in-law, it becomes clear that Ak'ko is actually not as powerless and voiceless as she might seem (figure 2.1). Ak'ko's four strategies for getting along with her mother-in-law are as follows: always ask her for guidance; always be sure to thank her for helping out; always try to include her in family activities; always apologize to her immediately when she scolds you. She then outlines the three important don'ts to maintain the good relationship: don't sulk, don't get angry, and don't

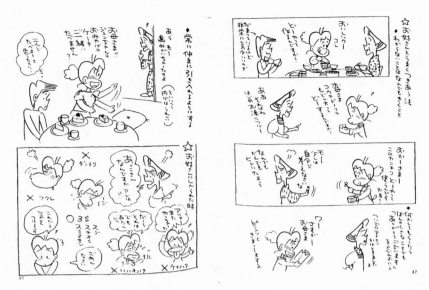

Source: Mitsuhashi, Chikako (1996), *Hāi Ak'ko desu 1* (Tokyo: Asahi Shinbunsha, 1996), pp. 42–43.

Figure 2.1   *Hi, I'm Ak'ko*: A Menacing Mother-in-law of the 1980s.

make any excuses. The reader comes to realize here that the key to getting along in the Sakamoto family is actually in Ak'ko's hands. Ak'ko can mastermind behind the scenes, deliberately keeping her head low at tense times to privilege the elder woman. Indeed, Ak'ko is the shaper of her mother-in-law's authority and domestic harmony, by cleverly deploying her own submissiveness. She can play dumb to her mother-in-law just like Michiko does to Granny, but Ak'ko's submissiveness is presented here as her own prudent choice.

By the 1990s, newspaper comics depicted in-law relations with noticeably less emphasis on hierarchy than in previous decades. In part because family relationships were now expected to be more fluid and negotiable across age and gender lines, illustrations of open conflict in family comics like *My Neighbors Yamada* became more commonplace. For example, an episode of *My Neighbors Yamada* is devoted to a dispute among three generations of the family over who is the boss (figure 2.2). Grandma Shige reminds the family that she is unequivocally the one who owns the title of the land for their house. But Takashi, her son-in-law, retorts that he is the one who paid for the house. Daughter Matsuko and grandson Noboru take turns to mediate this dispute but to no avail. Finally, Noboru puts an end to the contest by declaring that it's a pointless dispute because someday he is going to own it all anyway. This competition in the family mocks the erstwhile system of assigning authority by family position and suggests that power is distributed now according to diverse criteria: the mother-in-law has the financial power, the middle-aged son-in-law has the earning power, and the grandson has the advantage of youth. In this family, authority is neither invested in a patriarch or matriarch, nor fixed by seniority and gender; family members struggle with one another to gain the upper hand, because no one appears to have an automatic claim to it.

A comparison of these three episodes offers some insight into the changing images of the family that appeared in the *Asahi* comics over

Source: *Asahi* Newspaper, October 15, 1991.

Figure 2.2 *My Neighbors Yamada:* The Menacing Mother-in-law of the 1990s

the decades. The change is hardly breathtaking or revolutionary, but nevertheless points to the shifting expectations of gender roles and inter-generational relations over time. The change in women's family relations here mirrors the rising emphasis on motherhood that forced women's domestic role to shift from servicing in-laws to nurturing children (Allison 2000; Bernstein 1991). Accordingly, the place of elderly women in the "new" family also seemed to shift to the periphery where they would become relatively marginal to family activities. Even as domestic roles and values were reframed in an egalitarian language, however, the shift seemed contained firmly in the existing structure of the patriarchal order. The domestic sphere, no matter how "new" or "democratic" it appeared, was still the women's domain, a place where the roles and obligations had been reshuffled, without altering the gendered structure of control in the larger society.

Renegotiating Family Relationships

The influence of popular media, Michael Schudson reminds us, often depends on how it resonates with the readers' own experience (Schudson 1989). The world of newspaper comics must therefore parallel at some level the emotional realities of the readers to win their enduring affection. In this sense, the stories of the fictive families that unfolded in the *Asahi* from the 1970s through the 1990s seemed to capture the general apprehensions over changing expectations of family life in the burgeoning middle class. Such stories often addressed the unmistakable tensions of shifting hierarchical authority by exposing the mismatched expectations of family members to comic effect. In the daily life of readers, however, those same mismatches were not always as comical.

In the letters to the editor in the late 1980s, *Asahi*'s readers wrote about their resentments and disappointments over incompatible expectations in their family life.[7] In the case of mother/daughters-in-law relations, readers seemed to assume that new choices would release them from traditional roles, yet despaired when the release failed to materialize. In these conflicts, both sides seemed to feel hostage, and usually saw the other as unreasonable, unjust, self-serving and exploitative. As a result, typical accounts revealed intense bitterness:

> I've given my daughter-in-law so much support. . . . I was ex-hausted helping her out with the two children when she was sick this year. I even took time off from my work and went to stay over. So when I found out that she'd sent a [year-end] gift

to her own parents but not to me, [I felt treated] like a dirty
old rag...

(A homemaker in Tokyo, aged 58)[8]

I've now been married for three years to my husband who is a
civil servant, but I'm still astonished by the treatment I receive
as a *"yome* of the eldest son."* [Whenever we visit], I'm treated
simply as a labor hand, working from morning till night, eating
less at dinner, and taking the bath after everyone else.... I was
pregnant last year, but they still made me work all day from
five o'clock in the morning—to cook, wash and weed. I miscar-
ried after that... and then my patience ran out.... I've lost all
intentions of living with them in the future.

(A housewife in Yokohama City, aged 28)[9]

The accounts point to the unfulfilled aspirations for new roles and
relationships espoused by the readers at the time. Expecting to secure
more independence and respect from their in-laws, the older woman
was frustrated by the failure, and the younger woman was crushed by
the high price she paid. These women, and others like them, struggled
to control their relationships as the ground rules shifted, but ultimately
failed to renegotiate them meaningfully. They seemed eager to achieve
the ideal democratic relationships, yet botched those attempts like some
characters in the popular comics at the time.

From *Sazae-san* to *Earth Defense Family*, newspaper comics presented
in this chapter proved to be inherently conservative, hardly a medium suited
to promote radical change. Newspaper cartoons, on the whole, tend to
stay within prescribed limits to depict safe, amusing tales of domestic life
to appeal to a wide national readership. But within those limits, they can
often point poignantly to the contradictions and apprehensions of everyday
life in the existing social order (Hashimoto 2004a). Those contradictions
of the contemporary family are numerous: women's economic dependence
in the affluent middle-class; ideals of freedom within limits of domestic
boundaries; aspirations for change confined in prescribed transformations;
and coexisting ideologies of egalitarian democracy and patriarchy. Contemporary Japanese families continue to weave a tapestry of premodern,
modern, and postmodern elements into a synthetic model, embracing those
contradictions and defying linear transformations. If late modernity indeed
brings democratization to gender and family relationships, as Anthony
Giddens (1992) claims, then its application to the ongoing transformation
of Japanese families is not a straightforward one.

Notes

Blondie, Sazae, and Their Storied Successors

This paper has benefited from helpful comments by David Barnard, Hiroshi Nara, Nina Sadd, Gabriella Lukacs, and John Traphagan. I am also grateful for encouragement from William Kelly, and feedback from anonymous reviewers. Yasumasa Komori and the Japan Information Center of the University of Pittsburgh provided valuable research assistance.

1. Japan's first national census was carried out in 1920. The proportion of nuclear households was 54 percent of total households at that time.

2. The average has been about 2.2 per couple over the past decades.

3. I have excluded in this analysis two popular comic series published in the *Asahi* newspaper which were mainly about the workplace rather than the family — *Fuji Santarō* (1965–1991), and *Pēsuke* (1979–1993).

4. Originally, Sazae and Granny lived in the same neighborhood.

5. Ishii, *Nono-chan*, and *Tonari no Yamada-kun*, 2002a, 2002b.

6. Ishii is well-known for his work, *Ganbare Tabuchi-kun* which was modeled on the Hanshin Tigers baseball player Tabuchi Koichi. A reincarnation of this player appears in *My Neighbors* as a Physical Education teacher named Tabuchi.

7. Asahi Shinbun Tēma Danwashitsu. *Kazoku : Nihonjin no kazokukan* (Tokyo: Asahi Sonorama, 1988). I have used here a sample of fifty letters on in-law relationships that appeared in the column collected in chapter 4. The majority of them were written by daughters-in-law who reported poor, conflictive relationships. A handful of them were nurturing, loving in-law relationships, but interestingly, they involved mothers-in-law who had already died. A few men who were sandwiched between their mothers and wives also lent their voices to the column, attesting to the incompatible relations at home. The letters in this discussion are, of course, not meant to be representative of all newspaper readers, but a subset written by those who sent them to the editor.

8. Asahi Shinbun Tēma Danwashitsu. *Kazoku : Nihonjin no kazokukan*, pp. 360–61 (My translation).

9. Asahi Shinbun Tēma Danwashitsu. *Kazoku : Nihonjin no kazokukan*, pp. 365–66 (My translation).

Chapter 3

From Spiritual Fathers to Tokyo Godfathers

Depictions of the Family in Japanese Animation

Susan J. Napier

The 1991 animated film *Rōjin Z* directed by Kitakubo Hiroyuki but with a screenplay by Otomo Katsuhiro, one of the most famous directors in contemporary Japanese animation, contains a wealth of memorable images. One of the most arresting of these occurs early in the film: on an auditorium stage an inert elderly man, Takazawa Kijuro, lies on an enormous mechanical bed while beside him a younger man in a suit (whom the viewer later learns is Terada, a Ministry of Health official), explains the bed's peculiar virtues. Prefacing his explanation, Terada announces that "Society today is being crushed by a massive burden: the problem of the elderly." Then Terada asks, "How far are we willing to go to preserve our elders?"

Apparently very far indeed if by "preserve" Terada means "creating a technological environment that will keep the elderly alive." For the bed is, in fact, an entire world of family, domestic care, and entertainment all rolled into one. Powered by a nuclear chip, the bed/machine takes over all human duties including the most unpleasant. As the stunned audience watches, the bed covers the old man in sheets of water, scrubs him down and dries him off. Even the most sensitive bodily needs are taken care of. As a strange funnel shaped device with the logo "Toto" inscribed on it attaches itself briefly to Mr. Takazawa's genitals, Terada booms "Excretion—the most socially embarrassing problem of the old, causing the young bride or grandchild to avert their faces." But the bed is not simply a hygienic device. As Terada goes on to explain, it is

33

also a home entertainment center, allowing the elderly to buy and sell stocks, bet on the races, and chat with friends by phone. If the elderly person has no friends, it will even create a simulated personality to act as a conversation partner.

The audience is impressed but Haruko, Mr. Takazawa's home help nurse, is less so, and she becomes increasingly concerned when she begins to receive messages on her computer screen saying, "Help Me." Correctly divining that these messages are from Mr. Takazawa, speaking through the bed, Haruko and her fellow medical aides attempt to rescue him, only to find that the bed itself is working on a rescue mission. It has begun to evolve into a sentient being with a personality built on Mr. Takazawa's own memories, especially those of his late wife Haru.

The rest of the film consists of a memorable extended chase sequence as the bed, having taken on Haru's personality, makes a dramatic escape in an attempt to take Mr. Takazawa to the seaside resort of Kamakura, a place that seems to hold a particular emotional association for him. As Terada and his fellow government minions watch helplessly, the bed goes on a rampage, breaking out of the hospital, zooming through Tokyo and finally facing down another technological marvel—a machine that is similar in kind but programmed for purely military purposes, just outside the tunnel leading to Kamakura. Ultimately Mr. Takazawa's machine wins out but, initially it seems, at the cost of its own existence.

Mr. Takazawa, however, insists that he and his wife will meet again soon and he turns out to be correct, as the bed returns for him one more time. This final scene is the most spectacular in the film. On the rush through Tokyo, the bed had picked up numerous accretions, from traffic signs to steam shovels, but its final transformation is the most significant, for this time the bed has merged with Kamakura's most famous tourist attraction—a giant statue of the Buddha. Festooned with telegraph poles, the giant bed/Buddha/Haru looks down on Mr. Takazawa in his little apartment and intones, (in a lovely female voice),"I've come for you; shall we go to the sea dear?" The last image of the film is of the characters around Mr. Takazawa bowing their heads and clasping their hands in prayer.

For anime fans familiar only with Otomo's darkly apocalyptic classic *Akira* (1988), *Rōjin Z* may come as a surprise. The animation is more minimal, the story line less complex, and the characters more evenly divided between male and female. Even more surprising is the focus on an elderly infirm character, in striking contrast to *Akira*'s concentration on youth. Perhaps most surprising of all is the relatively comic, satirical nature of the film. While *Akira* was almost oppressively serious with a disturbing ending, *Rōjin Z* is often anarchically funny with a surprisingly upbeat ending given its essentially dark subject matter.

But the two films have more in common than may at first appear. Both of them are set in a near future world where technology is used supposedly to ameliorate but actually to alienate the living conditions of the future citizenry. Both works contain savage critiques of a government that sacrifices the innocent for the purposes of increasing military power. And finally, both of them implicitly comment on the breakdown of the family. In *Akira*'s case, the youthful delinquents, who are the film's main subject, have been abandoned by their parents to a harsh reform school institution. Even more pitiable is the situation of *Akira*'s secondary characters, mutant children whose families handed them over to the government for psychic experimentation. Similarly, in *Rōjin Z*, Terada states that Mr. Takazawa's family has signed a waiver allowing him to be the guinea pig for the government's experiment.

Most significantly from the point of view of this paper, each film also offers a kind of pseudo-family in compensation for the alienation it describes. In *Akira*'s case, the boys form a gang in which an elder brother figure looks out for a younger.[1] In *Rōjin Z*'s story, it is the feminine presence which is highlighted in the form of the dead wife Haru and the nurse aide Haruko (it is likely that the similarity of names is deliberate, since both characters play roles that are simultaneously wifely and motherly).

I begin this paper with the example of *Rōjin* Z because in many ways it illustrates the unique manner in which the art of animation can comment on what is essentially a sociocultural problem. Even today, when anime is increasingly available, many American viewers of anime tend to think of the medium as being dominated by science fiction and fantasy genres, ones that are usually not thought of in relation to family dramas. In fact, however, anime ranges across a wide variety of genres, from historical dramas to romantic comedies in many of which the family—in some form or other—remains an important component. Even more intriguingly, and this is in interesting contrast to its American counterpart, the ubiquitous animated science fiction and fantasy genres offer a surprising number of texts in which the family plays an important, even sometimes a dominant role.

Indeed, I would argue that science fiction and fantasy texts are particularly interesting showcases for the discussion of the family precisely because the genres defamiliarize common issues such as intergenerational conflict, sibling rivalry and even, as we saw in the case of *Rōjin Z*, geriatric problems, giving them a fresh spin by treating them outside the more traditional contexts of "home dramas."[2] As I have suggested elsewhere, the very nature of the animated medium, which deals explicitly with a nonrepresentational form of the "real," can offer more creative and perhaps even more intellectually stimulating explorations of common sociocultural issues than live action film or television can, precisely because of the freedom of imagery and imagination that animation gives access to.[3]

Thus, in the case of *Rōjin* Z, its blend of science fiction and fantasy helps to problematize the issue of elderly care in a particularly fresh and vivid way. The image of the technological bed that provides not only health treatments but even a simulated friend is a chilling vision of the anomie that may end up resulting from contemporary technological breakthroughs, breakthroughs that help our physical functioning but provide no emotional sustenance. This is underscored by Terada's mentioning of the "young bride or grandchild" who "avert their faces" from the bodily functions of the elderly. Although such a reaction to excretion is entirely understandable, the notion of "averting the face" *(kao o somukeru*—this is not translated in the English dialogue), implicitly suggests the tendency of society as a whole to try to look away at the increasing dehumanization of old age. In a live action home drama, this situation might be resolved by having the young people learn the joys of self-sacrifice in caring for an older person and in fact, there is a drama that shows exactly that outcome, although it is arguable how "realistic" such a scenario actually is in today's Japan.[4] In Otomo's parodic science fiction vision, however, such a wished for outcome is seen as unlikely—in fact, we never see Mr. Takazawa's family at all. Instead the film offers us the grotesque but perhaps strangely comforting vision of a machine that becomes more human and more spiritual than most of the people around it, reaching its literal apotheosis in the figure of the great Buddha as technological wife and mother, promising her "husband "a trip to the sea."

The film's vision of an impotent male and a ghostly wife/mother figure is also worth examining because in many ways it encapsulates some of the more disturbing trends associated with the Japanese family in recent decades. In my work on postwar Japanese literature, I have noted the increasing frequency of what I call the "absent woman" character in Japanese fiction by males and the growing powerlessness of the father figure in both literature and popular culture as well.[5] This trend seems clearly related to external developments in Japanese society. Already in the early decades following the war, commentators noted the effects of the demise of the *ie*, the traditional patriarchal household that had been outlawed by the U.S. Occupation. The loss of the father's traditional authority gave rise to a transformation in gender and family roles, echoed in film and popular culture, with an increasing emphasis on the younger generation and a concomitant vision of the father as a helpless, sometimes comically useless outsider figure. Sato Tadao chronicles many examples of the impotent father in feature films from the 1960s on and this trend seeped into animation as well. For example, the popular 1980s cartoon *Tensai Bakabon* featured a buffoonish father who became the butt of many jokes.

It is also in the 1980s that another trend begins to surface in popular culture, that of the absent woman, or more specifically the absent (or inadequate)mother. In live-action cinema, for example, the brilliant black comedy *Kazoku Gēmu* (Family Game), revealed a dysfunctional family with both an inadequate mother and a powerless father, but the copious anger on display in the film seems particularly directed towards the mother who appears incapable of sustaining the emotional needs of her sons. In the animated medium, creators as disparate as Miyazaki Hayao and Takahashi Rumiko, produced an immense number of popular series and films in which the mother is either absent or inadequate.

The reasons behind this trend in portraying what are essentially dysfunctional families are not hard to locate. The dismantling of the *ie* is of course a fundamental catalyst for change but in the recent decades it has been the changing value system of women, especially younger women, which has caused enormous repercussions throughout Japanese society. Perhaps the most significant change has been the increasing postponement of marriage and childbearing and, perhaps even more importantly, the reasons behind this change. Part of the reason must surely be the rise of a consumer culture in which freedom from constraint became a value in itself, leading many young women to resist entering traditional marriages where their lives would inevitably become more restricted. In fact, according to a 1994 survey, Japanese women were considerably less likely to see marriage as beneficial, in comparison to both Japanese men and American women.[6] Compared to the prewar (and even immediate postwar) emphasis on sacrifice for the family or the collectivity, the new values embraced by Japanese women seem to be ones emphasizing autonomy and individual satisfaction.

The new postwar culture that gave rise to these changes did not only influence women's values. It is clear that such factors as the rise and fall of the 1980s bubble economy, the rise of new technology—especially the dramatic rise of personal computer and cell phone use in the 1990s seem increasingly to be contributing to what David Gauntlett (2003) describes as "the transformation and detraditionalization of Japanese society."[7] The rest of this paper will trace this "transformation and detraditionalization" in relation to how the "family" is depicted in Japanese animation from the 1970s to the present. I place the word "family" in quotation marks because one finding of my research has been the amorphousness of the family unit as it is depicted in anime. In fact, while much of the anime I discuss shows an increasingly dark trend in depicting the family, a few more recent anime such as *Spirited Away* (Sen to Chihiro no kamikakushi), and *Tokyo Godfathers* (Tokyo Goddofāzāzu—the title is the same in Japanese), while showing the problems with the traditional family unit, also demonstrate attempts to construct what might be called a pseudo-family or even a pseudo*ie.*

In fact, the notion of a pseudo-family is not new. Even as far back as the 1970s, we can find what might be called an *"ie* equivalent" in the immensely popular series of films collectively known as the *Yamato* series. The 1978 *Farewell Yamato* (Saraba Uchūsenkan Yamato) and its many sequels is seen by most critics as the film that really launched the anime boom in Japan but for our purposes it is useful to examine it for its intriguing depiction of its crew members recreating a kind of household in space. Although technically set in the far future, *Yamato* is in many ways a science fiction reworking of the defeat in World War II, this time with a happy ending in which the spaceship *Yamato* (named for the battleship that was sunk off Okinawa in the last days of the war) becomes an agent for love and peace in the galaxy. *Yamato*'s amalgamation of prewar conservative values with postwar modernity can be seen in the constitution of the ship's crew which, I would argue, is in certain ways reminiscent of the ideals of the prewar *ie* system.

Thus, in *Farewell Yamato* themes such as sacrifice for the collectivity and spiritual continuity through one's ancestors are stressed. In one memorable scene, the stalwart young captain, Susumu Kodai is uncertain what to do in a confrontation with an evil, all consuming "white comet" that lies in his path Standing apprehensively on the ship's bridge, he is suddenly joined by the spirits of former Yamato captains who advise him on his next move and ultimately help him come to the decision that he must sail the Yamato into the comet alone, an act that may possibly save the Earth through destroying the comet, but will certainly result in his own destruction. In the movie's memorable final scene, Susumu sails the ship into the comet but he is actually not alone—he is accompanied by the body of his girlfriend Yuki, whose nurturing presence had made her the mother figure of the spaceship until her untimely death.

These two scenes to my mind emblemize the complex situation of the family in Japan in the 1970s continuing into the 1980s. On the one hand, Susumu's easy connection with his spiritual ancestors (the ghost captains), suggest his link to the traditional Japanese patriarchy. These ghosts are clearly father figures whose guidance from the past sustains Susumu at a difficult moment. On the other hand, the death of Yuki seems to prefigure the absent mother phenomenon of the decades to come.

Yuki's presence as a corpse is significant here since it is clearly depicted in a positive light. Her corpse may be seen as the physical manifestation of the memory of a nurturing mother figure, a figure who will become increasingly absent as time goes on.

Undoubtedly, *Yamato's* popularity rested on a variety of elements, most obviously the science fiction film boom of the 1970s, but its evocation of an essentially traditional "family" structure must surely have resonated during a period when the postwar generation of children had begun to grow up and question many of the values that had led Japan by the late 1960s to its first major wave of prosperity, only to have these values appear vulnerable as the result of various economic shocks in the early 1970s. The *Yamato* series (which actually began as a television series some years earlier), seems to embody this ambivalent moment when much of Japan still looked forward to a brighter future, emblematized by the *Yamato's* peaceful mission, but also were increasingly aware of the fading of traditional values, traditions that *Yamato* tellingly embodies as "ghosts" of the father and a corpse of a nurturing female.

This implicit concern about the fading of tradition seems to have continued into the 1980s and may be seen as embodied in one of the major popular culture phenomena of the era, Takahashi Rumiko's romantic fantasy *Ranma 1/2*, a *manga* and *anime* series that also seems to exist in slightly uneasy limbo between a traditional past and a motherless present. Like *Yamato*, *Ranma 1/2* harks back to the traditional *ie*, in this case in the form of its mise-en-scène, a *dōjō* (martial arts hall) run by the Tendō family. As Mr. Tendō proudly states in the opening episode of the series, the *dōjō* has been in the family for generations but, he laments, there is no male heir now to inherit it. Despite the fact that he has three able daughters, one of whom—the tomboy Akane—is exceptionally proficient in the martial arts, Mr. Tendō eagerly awaits the arrival of Ranma, the son of his best friend, whom he hopes to marry off to one of his daughters, a traditional Japanese method of securing the continuity of the family line. Unfortunately for Tendō, Ranma, who is training at a hot springs resort in China, has fallen into a magic spring which turns him into a girl when splashed with cold water (his father, who has also fallen into a spring, turns into a panda under similar conditions), but when splashed with warm water he turns back into a boy. This development leads to all manner of sexual and romantic hijinks as Mr. Tendō tries to continue seeing him as a boy, a blindness which amuses and shocks his daughters. As for Ranma himself, he desires desperately to return to a 100 percent masculine state but is continually thwarted.

Although very funny, *Ranma 1/2* also contains a more serious subtext, for example, the attack on fixed traditions and identity caused by the changes in contemporary Japanese society. The fact that these threats are depicted within a particularly traditional family situation (the *dōjō*) makes them even more noticeable. Written by a woman, who, in interviews at least, appears to be a very independent personality, *Ranma 1/2* in some ways seems to want to be both traditional and modern. On the one hand, it privileges Akane's assertive and lively personality and shows her demonstrating her scorn for boys/marriage/tradition through her many brilliant martial arts feats. Furthermore, certain episodes of the long running series, seems to suggest that Ranma is actually learning something by his constant immersion in femininity. Akane and Ranma can, in this interpretation, be seen as progressive role models. It should be noted, however, that from the point of view of her family, Akane's tomboyishness is seen as selfish and strange, very similar to the view that Japanese society seems to hold towards the young women who do not want to marry or have children. As for Ranma, his occasional forays into understanding his feminine side are usually quickly matched by his return to his almost hypermasculine martial arts fighter personality.

Looked at from the point of view of the depiction of the family in general, the household of *Ranma 1/2* exemplifies the new postwar reality in which the old certitudes no longer apply. The Tendō's traditional style house and pond are constantly the site of generational conflict between Ranma and his father, and gender battles between Ranma and Akane. In contrast to the traditional *ie* where the male head of the family technically held unquestioned authority, none of the fathers or father figures in the series are impressive. Ranma's father whether in panda or human form is alternately passive or cranky, while Mr. Tendō, the supposed head of the *dōjō,* is unperceptive, egotistical, and generally ineffective. Even the two fathers' master martial arts teacher, an old man named Happosai, while a powerful fighter, is more often characterized as a comically pathetic dirty old man. Moreover, the household has no mother, although Akane's sweet older sister tries to act as a substitute. The Tendō family is thus essentially an *ie* with its two basic pillars, the strong father and the always present mother, removed.

Perhaps most threatening of all is the alien figure of Ranma him/herself who is supposed to rescue the household but only makes it more vulnerable through his/her inability to hold onto a stable sexual identity. Far from being the traditional adopted son in law (*muko*) whose adoption helps the family maintain continuity, Ranma's appearance ushers chaos into the household. The sexual transgressiveness of Ranma's dual nature in relation to the powerless Mr. Tendō, the Tendō family's absent mother and Akane's tomboyishness all suggest a deep disequilibrium at the heart of the family structure.

In the fantasy realm of *Ranma 1/2*, the destabilization of the family is played out as comic, even perhaps cathartic, as we watch Ranma and his father throwing each other into ponds or Akane taking on all her male suitors and vanquishing them with her superior martial arts capability. By the mid-1990s, however, even Takahashi's comic vision had darkened considerably, as exemplified by her later series such as *Mermaid's Scar*, or *InuYasha*. On the science fiction front, however, the depiction of the dysfunctional family reached its acme (or perhaps its nadir), in two landmark series—*Neon Genesis Evangelion* (*Shinseiki Ebuangerion*), and *Serial Experiments Lain* (the English title is used). While the explicit theme of both these works appears to be the danger (and sometimes the allure) of technology, their real focus is on the disintegrating family unit, exemplified by a vividly demonstrated alienation between the generations and the marked inability of the main characters (in both cases young adolescents), to achieve any sort of emotional nurturance from the traditional family.

Turning first to *Evangelion*, it is important to note, as I have mentioned elsewhere, that one of the strengths of the series (and the two feature films) is how it uses the trappings of a conventional plucky-youths-defending-the-Earth-against-attacking-aliens scenario (as exemplified in the *Yamato* series), to create a riveting psychodrama of a society in crisis. This combination is evident from the very first episode as Shinji, the fourteen-year-old protagonist arrives alone at a near future Tokyo train station to join his father, the famous scientist Ikari Gendō. Shinji is not picked up by Ikari, however, but rather by the beautiful young Misato Katsuragi, who eventually takes on the dual role of mother figure /unattainable love interest as the series continues. Shinji, his father, and Misato, as well as a host of other characters connected with the secret headquarters known only as NERV, are on a mission to protect the Earth from the bizarre alien invaders known as the Angels.

As the series unfolds, however, it becomes clear that the humans, all of whom carry enormous psychological baggage, are at least as threatening (to themselves and sometimes to each other), as the Angels. This baggage, we are led to believe, is largely due to parental transgression, for the series shows a plethora of dysfunctional parents. Shinji's mother is dead and his relationship with his chilly scientist father is characterized by intense mutual distaste. Misato also bears psychological scars from her relationship with her father which cause her to act out towards men in unhealthy ways. Misato's superior, Ritsuko Miyagi so despises her mother that, in an extraordinary scene, she jabs what's left of her mother's computerized brain with a sharp needle, commenting, "I never did like my mother." Shinji's fourteen-year-old female teammate, the angry Asuka Langley, bears perhaps the heaviest burden of all—her mother's suicide by hanging.

In the series controversial final episodes, the viewer enters the mind of Shinji and those of several of the other main characters to discover a form of a mental interrogation taking place. Asked what he is most afraid of, Shinji does not answer "the Angels" but instead first replies "Myself," then "Others," and finally, "My father." Shinji's teammates give similarly grim responses: Misato finds herself unable to escape from her hatred towards her father while Asuka is tormented by images of her mother's suicide and what appears to be her father's emotional abandonment of the two of them.

Although it is the father's absence and inadequacy that is explicitly highlighted in the series, it is possible to argue that the absent mother is at least as important. While Shinji's mother is technically dead, she actually returns in several forms. The most fundamental one is that of the EVA, the giant robots with which Shinji and his fourteen-year-old teammates, the so-called children (the English term is used), merge in order to attack the Angels. The EVA's maternality is made clear from the opening episode when Shinji is forced to climb into "his" EVA inside NERV headquarters. While NERV technicians shout the order to unlock the "umbilical bridge" (the English term is used), Shinji in a scene slightly reminiscent of the bath imagery in *Rōjin Z* finds himself immersed in fluid inside the EVA. After this metaphoric "birth scene," Shinji is found to "synchronize" with his EVA at an extraordinarily high level. The EVA's maternality is underscored in Shinji's first fight with the Angel when he appears to have been knocked out by the Angel and all contact is lost between him and the anxious bystanders at NERV. Just when it appears that the Angel will triumph, however, Shinji's EVA starts to revive without his conscious control and subdues the Angel in a brutal confrontation. In this scene, the viewer is clearly meant to see the EVA as protecting Shinji, as a mother would a child.

The Japanese critic Kotani Mari has argued that *Evangelion* is a "family romance" in which NERV symbolizes the patriarchy.[8] Using this interpretation, Ikari Gendō is clearly the head of the *ie*. His orders are never questioned by his subordinates and it makes sense that he brings back his only son to serve the needs of the collectivity. But if NERV is an *ie*, it is an overtly dysfunctional one, under attack from both inside and out. The outer attackers include not only the Angels who serve as the alien Other, but also another secret human headquarters significantly called SEELE (the German word for Soul), also apparently run as a patriarchal organization. In the final apocalyptic battles, it is actually SEELE that destroys NERV, an example, perhaps, of the patriarchy at war with itself. Even more disturbing, however, is the spiritual malaise within NERV itself. Unlike the *Yamato* series, which has an outwardly similar narrative format, tradition, and continuity are shown as suspect in *Evangelion*. While Shinji is Gendō's actual son, he shows him none of the respect and love that Susumu exhibits towards his spiritual "fathers" aboard the *Yamato*. And while the past is clearly empowering in *Yamato*, as the spaceship's iconic name suggests, in *Evangelion*, the past becomes personal and suffocating, with virtually all the characters attempting to escape their haunted childhoods.

Even more subversive is the role of the female/maternal presence in *Evangelion*. While Susumu's dead girlfriend Yuki in *Yamato* suggests the incipient absence of the nurturing female, her body is still there and Susumu is comforted by memories of her nurturing presence (another instance where the past is seen as beneficial in the *Yamato* series). In contrast, *Evangelion* portrays the female, especially the mother, in often problematic ways, as fundamentally failing to perform their maternal duties. Asuka's mother abandons her through suicide while Ritsuko's mother provokes only contempt. Most disturbing perhaps is Shinji's dead mother. It is revealed toward the end of the series that Shinji's father has had her essentially cloned into the identity of Shinji's other female teammate, Ayanami Rei but, unlike the dead body of Yuki, Rei offers no reassuring emotional nurturance to Shinji—indeed she is perhaps the most distant and disturbing character in the entire series, seemingly constituted only out of lack and negativity, a passive puppet to Shinji's father's machinations. Even the EVA's ultimately fail the "children," allowing STEELE's version of the machines to overpower them.

The film and television series end differently and it is worth discussing some of their differences. In the case of the series, Shinji is given a glimpse of another version of his life in which his mother is still alive living harmoniously with his father. In marked contrast, the film ends with a hyperbolically apocalyptic finish, including an extraordinary scene of a gigantic Ayanami Rei who stretches across the universe as fiery crosses merge into her immaterial body. Only Shinji is unable to meld with her and the viewer's final glimpse of him is with Asuka alone in a vast wasteland, perhaps in a potential Adam and Eve scenario although Asuka's last words in the film are "I feel sick," hardly an upbeat way to end. Furthermore, if Rei can be equated with Shinji's mother, then her repudiation of him is notably disturbing. *Evangelion*'s film version thus ends with a vision of dysfunctional solitude towards which the family can provide no emotional compensation. Indeed, both film and TV series seem to be suggesting that it is the family itself that is the problem.

After this bleak depiction, it is hard to imagine a more disturbing view of the modern family, but my next example, *Serial Experiments Lain*, surpasses even *Evangelion* in its utter nihilism. I have described *Lain* elsewhere as a "home drama invaded by the surreality of cyberculture" but for the purposes of this paper, I will focus on the home drama aspect.[9] Set in the near future, *Lain* concerns a middle-school student who, when first encountered, appears to live in a typical Japanese family consisting of her mother, father, and older sister. Initially, the only unusual aspect of her family seems to be her father's inordinate fascination with computer technology. Eventually, he persuades Lain to join him in his obsession, giving her an elaborate computer known as a NAVI. Lain is soon drawn into the world of the computer, known as the WIRED, and increasingly bizarre events take place both inside and outside the WIRED. As a result, Lain grows more and more alienated in both worlds. Her family does little to help her. At one point her mother simply turns away when Lain is about to ask a question and her father seems increasingly immersed in his own solipsistic technological realm.

The series ends with a variety of dark revelations. In one of the more disturbing scenes, Lain comes home to find that her family appears to have simply left, leaving her alone in a chilly looking environment whose affectlessness is heightened by the flat lines and cold blues and grays of the animation itself. Eventually Lain learns the truth—she has no family and never had one. She is simply a piece of software who must cancel herself for the sake of the rest of the world. Although she sees her "father" once again, this time in the realm of the WIRED, he offers her an essentially imaginary future, one in which they will have tea and "madeleine" cookies together. The "madeleines" are of course a reference to Proust's *Remembrance of Things Past*, but they are a deeply ironic one. Whereas Proust's work was all about memory and the family and the individual's complex connection with both, *Lain* is a vision of nonconnection in a technological nightmare in which neither family nor the individual exists any longer.

Lain was broadcast in the late 1990s in Japan and seems very much a dark comment on the rise of Japanese cyberculture (s) that was occurring during that period as more and more individuals found their own WIRED worlds which, for some, competed with the "real" worlds of family and community. Some commentators saw the spread of what Todd Holden and Takako Tsuruki call "new cultures of encounter" to be a positive, "outward reaching " phenomenon, but other critics drew harsh comparisons between the contemporary world and previous forms of social bonding. Holden and Tsuruki quote a Japanese commentator, T. Kogawa who suggests that "as far as the present Japanese collectivity is concerned, it is electronic and very temporal, rather than a conventional, continuous collectivity based on language, race, religion, region, or taste."[10]

My two final examples of the family in Japanese anime, the 2001 *Spirited Away* and the 2003 *Tokyo Godfathers* may almost be seen as implicit responses to the previous statement. On the one hand the films portray not only a Japan of alienated and fragmented families, but also they show attempts at compensation for this condition. In the fantasy *Spirited Away*'s case the condition is countered by the example of a pseudo-*ie* a magical bathhouse for the gods that is very clearly related to the notion of a "continuous collectivity" based on "language, race, religion, region, and taste." The more realistic *Tokyo Godfathers* is at times more radical, suggesting the possibility of new forms of the family in which the sexes no longer have defined roles, but in the end it also upholds the notion of the traditional family, although one that is tempered through a variety of traumatic but enlightening experiences on the part of the members.

Turning first to *Spirited Away*, it is worth mentioning that the film is a product of the great animation director Miyazaki Hayao, whose films, throughout the years, have often centered on the family or occasionally (in the case of *Kiki's Delivery Service*, for example) a compensatory form of pseudo family. While generally upbeat and warm, it should be noted that many of Miyazaki's films center around orphans or children with only one parent (almost always the father, with the exception of his most recent film *Howl's Moving Castle*). While this aspect may be related to the fact that Miyazaki's own mother was away in hospital with tuberculosis for a good part of his childhood, it also may have something to do with the fact that Miyazaki's Studio Ghibli began producing films in the 1980s, a period when the trope of the absent mother began to manifest itself in Japanese popular culture. That being said, it is important to remember that the mother, even if absent as in *My Neighbour Totoro* (Tonari no Totoro) or *Kiki's Delivery Service* (Majo no Takkyūbin), is always regarded affectionately by her offspring. Furthermore, the father in the Miyazaki's eighties and nineties films is more often present than the mother (*Totoro, Nausicaä*), and is also appealingly presented. In fact the consistent depiction of warm family relationships in Miyazaki's films strongly suggests a form of compensation for the turbulent changes that were occurring in Japanese society during that period.

For this reason the largely negative portrayal of the family in *Spirited Away* is particularly intriguing. *Spirited Away* centers around a young girl named Chihiro who, in contrast to all previous Miyazaki heroines, is initially shown as sullen and apathetic. The depiction of the parents is equally negative: the father is seen as boorish and aggressive, while Chihiro's mother seems cold and uninterested. When a timorous Chihiro takes her mother's arm, for example, her mother's only response is to tell her not to "cling so." The parents are also reckless consumers, a trait metaphorically underlined by the movie's first fantastic twist, the transformation of the parents into pigs as they gorge themselves at a mysterious restaurant. The fact that it is up to Chihiro to rescue them, which she spends the rest of the movie doing, underlines the fact that, underneath the dazzling and inventive imagery, the movie's subtext is really about parental inadequacy and family fragmentation. Like Lain, Chihiro is alone in a strange realm. In fact the two even share the motif of fading away: *Lain* begins each episode with a song sung in English that includes the evocative refrain, "I am falling, I am fading." *Spirited Away* includes a scene early on in which Chihiro literally does begin to fade away until she is given a magic food by the mysterious youth Haku.

The trope of fading on the part of both young girl characters suggests a modern world without emotional or spiritual sustenance enough to maintain them. In *Lain* this vision is taken to its final limits with the viewer's last glimpse of Lain "fading" into the static of a black and white television set, representing the alien and alienating world of technology. In contrast, *Spirited Away* offers an alternative to "fading," a marvelously reimagined fantasy version of the traditional *ie*, the bathhouse of the gods to which Chihiro goes to find work in order to liberate her parents from the spell.

Much like the ideal of the prewar *ie*, the bathhouse is controlled by an elder with an iron hand and its inhabitants work for the sake of the larger collectivity and see themselves very much in terms of insider and outsider. (Chihiro, for example, is initially rejected because she is human.) Even the work that the bathhouse performs, bathing the Japanese spirits, is overtly connected with Japanese tradition. There are some significant differences, however. Most importantly, the bathhouse is controlled by a woman, a witchlike figure known as Yubaba. Furthermore, most of the major figures in the film are female. Besides Chihiro and Yubaba, there are also Chihiro's mentor, Lin, and Yubaba's more kindly twin sister, Zenība. Even Haku, the major male character of the film is notable for his androgynous features. It is possible that in this privileging of the feminine that Miyazaki is harking back to very early Japanese history when Japan apparently did have matriarchal rule, but it is also possible that Miyazaki is emphasizing the feminine within the collectivity precisely because of its increasing disappearance from the real world. From that point of view, the introduction, late in the film, of the kindly, even grandmotherly Zenība, who along with the elder sisterly Lin, are the characters who treat Chihiro with the most kindness may suggest Miyazaki's recognition of the need for "mothering" in an increasingly alienating environment.

Spirited Away is unique among Miyazaki's films in its portrayal of a contemporary society that is not only spiritually and emotional empty, but it also offers a vision of how to compensate for this. Chihiro's hard work and self-sacrifice lead to her quasi-adoption by the bathhouse/*ie* and her own ultimate empowerment. How much this empowerment will be retained when she returns to her real family is ambiguous. Perhaps Miyazaki's prescription for the health of the family as a whole would be for all three of them to work in the bathhouse. Whether or not this is a possibility, the viewer carries away from the film a sumptuously detailed vision of a household where connection still matters, a far cry from the alienating final images of *Lain* or *Evangelion*.

The director Kon Satoshi's latest film, *Tokyo Godfathers* also offers a richly imagined alternative to the loneliness and fragmentation of contemporary Japan but, in this case, his vision includes both new and traditional aspects. Very loosely based on the 1947 John Ford film, *Three Godfathers, Tokyo Godfathers* begins on Christmas night in downtown Tokyo where three homeless people, the grumpy alcoholic Gin, the sentimental transvestite Hana, and the angry young runaway, Miyuki, find an abandoned baby in the garbage. The film details the threesome's attempts to return the baby, whom they name Kiyoko, to her rightful parents, even as they each become attached to the child in their own distinctive way. Ultimately the baby becomes a deus ex machina catalyst for change. Gin confronts his own past pattern of running from responsibility and, in one of the film's many coincidences, is reunited with the daughter he abandoned years before. Miyuki opens up to her vulnerability and is reunited with her father and mother. Hana, perhaps the most interesting and affecting character in the group, has the most trouble giving up the baby but at the end seems resigned to returning to her life as an entertainer in a cozy transvestite bar.

Up until the end, however, the film's view of the traditional family is a bleak one. Gin is clearly an inadequate father whose drunkenness and gambling debts put his family into jeopardy. Miyuki remembers her mother as someone who spends all her days chanting the sutras, and her last memory of her father before she left home is of attacking him with a knife. Hana has apparently been cut off by her real family. Even less appealing are the couple whom the trio assume are baby Kiyoko's real parents, a shady, apathetic duo who do not seem to have the energy to keep their marriage alive. Furthermore, the society depicted around them is also a grim, forbidding place. The trio encounter a *yakuza* boss who gets shot, an impoverished neighborhood of Latin American immigrants, and in a particularly disturbing scene, Gin is viciously attacked by young toughs who boast of "cleaning up" the homeless. Like Miyazaki in *Spirited Away*, Kon has an explicit critical agenda, and the film does an excellent job of detailing the many ugly aspects of contemporary Japanese society.

Also like Miyazaki, however, Kon offers an alternative to this vision of urban anomie that is romantic, if not actually fantastic. True to its setting on Christmas night, the film revolves around many small miracles—Gin meeting his daughter unexpectedly, Miyuki seeing her father suddenly through a train window, and, in a final action sequence, the three of them saving baby Kiyoko from what appears to be certain death at the hands of a woman who had kidnapped her. The film ends with a vision of reconstituted families—even Hana goes back to her welcoming bar, that is in some ways conservative. Indeed, the emphasis on saving the baby and the joys of parenthood suggest an implicit critique of the young Japanese who postpone parenting. But the film also offers a more radical alternative to the traditional family which is its vision of the trio of homeless people themselves. Gin, Hana, and Miyuki constitute a new kind of family. Gin turns out to be a protective father to Miyuki, while Hana is a nurturing (if at times nagging) "wife" to Gin and a maternal presence for Miyuki. Miyuki, though often rebellious and sullen, learns by the end of the film to appreciate her surrogate "parents" and develops a more nurturing personality of her own.

Exploring over thirty years of anime depictions of the family, I would hesitate to make too many sweeping statements, simply because of the enormous variety and range of Japanese animation. Yet, a few themes might be suggested. The theme of the absent parent is one that underlines a vast number of anime, from the *Yamato* series through *Tokyo Godfathers*, as well as the theme of the increasing sense of the disintegration of the family, often tied to the rise of technology and the consumer society (*Rōjin Z*, *Evangelion*, *Lain*, *Spirited Away*, *Tokyo Godfathers*). However, all is not entirely bleak. Beginning with the *Yamato* series, we saw the development of what I call the "pseudo *ie*," a kind of family that is not constituted by blood relations but by shared work and emotional bonds. However, in the 1980s and 1990s such pseudofamilies become hard to find. *Ranma 1/2* for example, almost seems like a parody of the *ie*, showing it under extreme attack. *Rōjin Z*'s savage attack on using technology to substitute for family ultimately surprises us by giving as a solution the vision of the technological Buddha/Wife, a vision that could be either nihilistic or comforting. In *Evangelion* and *Lain* technology is clearly threatening to the family. *Evangelion*'s NERV is a site of despairing alienation and in *Lain* the family literally disappears into the maw of the Wired.

With the turn of the century, however, at least in the examples of *Tokyo Godfathers* and *Spirited Away*, the notion of family as a respite from the alienating outside world seems to have returned, but in a less simplistic fashion than in *Yamato*. Miyazaki and Kon do not turn a blind eye to the emptiness and brutality of contemporary culture, but they do offer what might be a praticeable alternative. Rather than basing this alternative on technological development as *Rōjin Z* does, the two films return to a celebration of human connection. Whether this celebration of connection will become a trend in future Japanese animation is impossible to say but the fact that *Spirited Away* was the highest grossing film in Japanese history and *Tokyo Godfathers* was extremely well reviewed suggest that their visions of alternatives to family fragmentation and social disintegration have at least struck a chord among the contemporary Japanese public.

Notes

From Spiritual Fathers to Tokyo Godfathers

1. Isolde Standish, "*Akira*, Post-modernism and Resistance," in *The Worlds of Japanese Popular Culture*, D. P. Martinez, ed. (Cambridge: Cambridge University Press, 1998), p. 67. In her commentary on *Akira*, Isolde Standish notes how the young adolescents in the film are shown as "being without the emotional clutter of the traditional extended family," but it is clear that within their new "pseudofamily" there is still a great deal of "emotional clutter."

2. Another interesting example of a genre defamiliarizing problems with the elderly is the recent (2002) live action horror film *Ju-on* (The Grudge). This unsettling but extremely popular work begins with a home health care worker's visit to a creepy domicile where she is expected to look after an elderly woman. Although the actual ghost of the film turns out to be the wife of the family, (in itself not only a nod to Japanese tradition, but also perhaps an evocation of the complex situation of married women in contemporary Japan), the scenes where the helper cleans up a (by Japanese standards), disgustingly untidy house and cares for the disoriented old woman are extremely disturbing. The film's juxtaposition of horror with old age is one that I am not aware of in any recent American horror films, suggesting that old age itself has become a condition evoking horror among contemporary Japanese.

3. See Susan J. Napier, "The Problem of Existence in Japanese Animation," *Bulletin of the American Philosophical Society* (March 2005).

4. See Andrew Painter, "The Telepresentation of Gender in Japan," in *Reimaging Japanese Women*, Imamura, ed. (Berkeley: University of California Press, 1996). In this essay Painter discusses a television home drama in which a career minded Japanese wife learns the satisfaction of taking care of her elderly mother-in-law, including cleaning up after her bowel movements.

5. See Susan J. Napier, *The Subversion of Modernity: The Fantastic in Modern Japanese Literature: The Subversion of Modernity* (London: Routledge, 1996).

6. Noriko Tsuya and Larry Bumpass, eds., *Marriage, Work and Family Life in Comparative Perspective: Japan, South Korea, and the United States* (Honolulu: University of Hawaii Press, 2004).

7. David Gauntlett, Preface to *Japanese Cybercultures*, eds., N. Gottleib and M. McLelland (London: Routledge, 2003), p. xiii.

8. Kotani Mari, *Seibo Ebuangerion* (Tokyo: Magazine House, 1997), p. 19.

9. For a discussion of *Evangelion* and *Lain* in relation to technology, see Susan J. Napier, "When the Machines Stop: Terminal Identities in Modern Japanese Animation," *Science Fiction Studies* (Fall 2002).

10. Todd Holden and Takako Tsuruki, "Deai-kei: Japan's New Culture of Encounter," in *Japanese Cybercultures*, N. Gottleib and M. McLelland, eds., p. 44.

Chapter 4

The Agony of Eldercare

Two Japanese Women Directors Study an Age-Old Problem

Keiko I. McDonald

Growing Awareness of Alzheimer's East and West

Alzheimer's disease and senile dementia have become household words East and West in recent years. Both could be described as a curse laid on the blessing of longevity that is increasingly a fact of life in developed countries like Japan and the United States. Japan begins the new century on an elderly note, with 18 percent of the population over the age of sixty-five. Women have a life expectancy of eighty-four, men of seventy-eight. Some 12.7 percent of Americans are over sixty-five, with a life expectancy nearing eighty for women, seventy-four for men. Statistical projections are difficult to correlate usefully, given two such different societies and approaches to health care, yet the challenges to both have much in common. Any disease of longevity at a time of increasing longevity is a matter of growing concern. Alzheimer's and senile dementia stand out because death comes by way of the most deeply personal and individual deterioration imaginable, and at a pace most often cruelly slow. What begins as a problem for the immediate family quickly escalates into a matter of concern for society at large. The patient loses liberty far in advance of life itself. Family and caregivers must deal with issues and interpretations accordingly. One might say that these diseases must be somehow socialized, even as the patient loses touch with personal and social identity.

Individuals, families, and society at large are all understandably concerned. According to the Japanese Ministry of Health, Labor and

Welfare, the number of Japanese senior citizens suffering from senile dementia reached 3.14 million in September 2002. Among them those afflicted with Alzheimer's are numbered 1.57 million.[1]

In the United States, the National Institutes of Health puts the number of Americans likely to suffer Alzheimer's after the age of eighty-five at 47 percent.[2] That grim forecast strikes home in a country where tens of millions have no health care coverage and costs for those who do are spiraling out of control. As a result, no one in this country's media-mediated culture is likely to escape exposure to the impending threat of a disease whose "inexorable dissolution of self" (Cohen and Eisdorfer 1986, 22) inflicts suffering and confusion on its victim, and on families and society as well.

The expansive (and expensive) reach of this horrifying life outcome appears to be getting its share of attention worldwide. In the United States, a convenient measure of that fact is that Alzheimer's has become a major growth industry. Madison Avenue is working overtime to evolve images and approaches that are both socially acceptable and compelling in the marketplace. The gifts and promises of research and remedy are also a presence in national politics. Results are predictably very much mixed to date, though the American belief in problem solving seems fully engaged, as does the equally characteristic appetite for true-life forensics. Celebrity victims and caretaker spokespersons abound. The testimonial literature is alive and well in all the expected forms and places.

A Sampling of Film Depictions

Cinema's close ties with contemporary life should make it the ideal venue for depicting a disease whose slow execution by loss of self puts the individual and society at odds in so many ways. Results of course will be culturally specific and therefore notably different East and West.

Filmmakers in the United States have worked in genres that range from straightforward documentary to boldly experimental horror. Bill Kersey's powerful *87 Topaz* (2004) documents a grandson's recollection of his grandfather's end of life decline and death from Alzheimer's. Renny Harlin's horror/thriller *Deep Blue Sea* (1999) features an Alzheimer's research team whose experimental sharks turn on them. Robert Ackerman's TV drama *Forget Me Never* (1999) casts Mia Farrow and Martin Sheen in a tale of memory loss suffered in middle age by an attorney wife/mother.

Japan's aging demographic put filmmakers on notice somewhat earlier than in the United States. *Kōkotsu no hito* [Twilight Years, 1973] came out before Alzheimer's had become a household name. Director Toyoda Shirō (1905–1977) was himself of an age to bring an extra measure of sensitivity to his painstaking depiction of a grandfather's need of care and understanding. Toyoda was famous for his faithful film adaptations of literary works (*bungei eiga*) so moviegoing readers of Ariyoshi Sawako's best-selling novel could count on a vivid portrayal of an urban family's struggle to live with the burden placed on it by a grandfather's entry into Alzheimer's twilight zone.

A very different sort of grandfather figures in Itō Shunya's *Hana Ichimonme* [A Song About Flowers, 1985]. He is an intellectual, a retired museum curator. The burden of his care falls chiefly on a daughter-in-law. Itō's less resigned approach yields a tragic ending more in tune with present-day doubts about the power of family to fend off the horrors of final helplessness.

Yoshida Yoshishige a.k.a. Yoshida Kijū (b. 1933) enters even darker territory in *Ningen no yakusoku* [The Promise, 1986]. His powerful study of progressive dementia shows the terrifying dilemma of euthanasia bringing anguish to two younger generations. Kuriyama Tomio (b. 1946) approaches Alzheimer's by way of black comedy in *Hōmu-suīto hōmu* [Home Sweet Home, 2000]. His afflicted paterfamilias is a former opera singer whose decline is both histrionically absurd and elaborately destructive of family life.

Japanese cinema's first century of directing, like centuries of Japanese culture generally, has been male-dominated, so is scarcely surprising that the films just mentioned are all by men and about male sufferers (with one exception). Just recently, Sasabe Kiyoshi (b. 1959) has studied marital relations in an interesting new context. *Han'ochi* [Pleading for Death, 2003] depicts the psychological torment of a policeman who finally yields to his wife's pleas for an end to her decline into Alzheimer's dementia.

The most recent addition to this genre is Tsutsumi Yukihiko's *Ashita no kioku* [Memories of Tomorrow, 2006] based on Ogiwara Hiroshi's novel of the same title. This film in chiefly domestic drama format concerns a middle-aged workaholic businessman (played by Watanabe Ken) who is stricken suddenly with a debilitating disease at the apex of his corporate career. Tutsumi foregoes the usual focus on the career and social consequences in favor of a probing and intelligent view of love and trust rekindled as husband and wife take refuge in mountains whose idyllic scenery underscores the peace they find through memories of the past given new life.

With very few exceptions, female filmmakers are a late twentieth century phenomenon in Japan, though as in other areas, numbers of talented individuals rose to the challenge as access to the director's chair became available. As might be expected, not a few of these newcomers came prepared with agendas supplied by rapid and sometimes radical social change in Japan. Two in particular responded to the problem of an aging population with thought-provoking studies of the problems of eldercare, especially those associated with dementia.

Still active in her seventies, Haneda Sumiko (b. 1929) is now recognized as one of Japan's leading women directors. She made her mark in documentaries. Her impressive roster of thirty titles includes four which studied eldercare between 1984 and 1999. The most notable, *Chihō-rōjin no kango* [How to Take Care of the Senile, 1984] was revised and rereleased later in the year under the title *Chihōsei rōjin no sekai* [The World of the Senile, 1984].

Matsui Hisako (b. 1946) made her debut in 1997 with a feature film *Yukie* [Solitude Point], an intensely dramatic view of suffering caused by Alzheimer's. She returned to that subject in 2002 with *Oriume*. Haneda's *The World of the Senile* and Matsui's *Oriume* stand out as the most dynamic explorations to date of old age in crisis. Both skillfully conjoin the pity and the horror of the victim's plight with the equally troubling and complex consequences for the family.

Given the overall theme of this volume—family conflict in contemporary Japan—it may be well to explain that works like these pose intriguing questions, which the film critic uses, in turn, to analyze and evaluate them. What, for example, is the salient feature of each director's treatment? Does she take an innovative approach to the family conflict engendered by the stressful complexities of caring for a victim of dementia? How does each resolve the ageless moral issue of filial obligation (*giri*) in conflict with personal inclination (*ninjō*)? Which mode of representation does the director choose? How does she generate the desired audience response?

The World of the Senile (1984): A Documentarian's Dramatic Method

The original eighty-three minute version of Haneda's *The World of the Senile* (1984) was an independent documentary. Three years had passed between shooting and release but the time for such a film had clearly come. Audiences flocked to over a thousand screenings nationwide.[3] Haneda noted later that hers was the first documentary to elicit "such an overwhelming response" (Haneda 2000, 117). One might ask why Haneda emerged from retirement to undertake a project whose subject might be thought depressing, even threatening, for a person her age.

Yet in 1982, she accepted a commission to make an educational film for doctors and nurses with a professional interest in its title subject: *How To Take Care of the Senile*. A groundbreaking book on the subject had been published the year before in the United States, *The 36-Hour Day* by Peter Rabins and Nancy Mace.

The revised, expanded version released in 1984 had a title more in keeping with the general audience it addressed: *The World of the Senile*. This project was a natural extension of Haneda's lifelong interest in the *kango* genre of films about nursing. It was also more deeply personal, as Haneda herself explained: "I have a latent desire to know more about old age. Most Japanese films have been concerned with childhood and youth, and there is hardly any work devoted to aging . . . especially the aging process reviewed by an old person . . ." (Haneda 2000, 189).

The World of the Senile offers case studies of five female patients in a forty-bed nursing home in Kumamoto Prefecture. All are to some degree victims of Alzheimer's or dementia. Yae and Sadako, eighty-four and seventy-four respectively, have had strokes. Both have suffered severe memory loss. Sadako has no awareness of who she is. Taka, in her seventies, suffered a cerebral hemorrhage which left her delusional. Her incessant monologue draws on garbled memories of a life of hardship in youth and as a young widow. Her chief delusional anxiety has to do with being still the family's sole breadwinner. Momoe, too, still lives in the past, haunted by youthful unhappiness. In her mind she is not a brooding eighty-three-year-old in a nursing home but an eighteen-year-old innocent berated by a stepmother unsympathetic to her menstrual problems. Tsue is a victim of Alzheimer's. She wanders from room to room, searching for her old home, carrying a paper bag filled with personal oddments.[4]

Scenes of nursing home life alternate with interviews as family members explain why they could no longer care for mothers or in-laws at home. The monotony of confinement is eased somewhat by crosscutting to the New Year's holiday which patients spend with family.

Like any documentarian, Haneda was concerned to give recorded reality a commanding presence on screen.[5] Even an audience interested in her subject could not be expected to endure undifferentiated exposure to the problematic dreariness of nursing home confinement. Some touches of human-interest drama must obviously come to the fore. Haneda explained her approach this way:

> Regarding the point of view, there is no boundary between fictional film and documentary. There is a documentary indefinitely close to "drama" and vice versa. Though I have been making

documentary films all my life, I use a dramatic method if I think it more appropriate to express my feelings and thoughts. I start by looking at reality and then choose imagery to present what I feel about it. . . . (Matsumoto 1996, 98)

Haneda's "dramatic method" is highly selective, even vigorously editorial where real-life detail is concerned. She readily admitted taking the "utmost care not to film the elderly in conditions of filth." Her audience is not asked to stomach the sordid disgrace of senescent minds and bodies losing all control. These old ladies aren't seen soiling themselves or attacking staff or one another. Even two views of diapering are notably discreet. The camera's observant gaze is fixed, not on the appalling extreme of helplessness itself, but on the helpfully compassionate interaction between nurse and patient.

Compassion lies at the heart of Haneda's dramatic method throughout. The staff, in her view, are unfailingly kind and patient, often with a suggestion of familial love. The film opens on that note. Shots of the night nurse on duty yield to others of her morning rounds. She greets Taka cheerfully and sets about changing her diaper, making small talk about the old lady's daughter Kayako. Taka says she doesn't have a daughter. A close-up, however, shows her look of contentment as the nurse deflects that doubt by saying that Taka will be clean in a jiffy. As the nurse passes on to the next two beds, she notices something amiss. "Where are your glasses?" she asks politely.

Haneda's Principle of Selectivity and Presentation of Conflict

Haneda described the nursing home's core philosophy this way in an interview: "If you continue to nurse with respect for patients' feelings and thoughts, symptoms of senility can be lessened though not eradicated" (Haneda 2000, 105). Human nature being what it is, the absence of even a single instance of caregiver anger or frustration speaks for a high degree of selectivity on the part of the director. Professionals and family alike exhibit a consistency of compassion that is, in fact, as natural in the Buddhist culture of Japan as unflinching forensic frankness would be in the American context. Still, Haneda's "dramatic" selectivity makes good documentary sense, given the need to appeal to a general audience early in the history of public awareness of Alzheimer's as an impending health crisis. A gloomy, conflicted atmosphere might well have disincentivized viewers in the early 1980s. Then too, participating families might have balked at signing releases vital to any documentary enterprise, for obvious reasons.[6]

Students of cinema will be aware of another more subtle effect of the director's selectivity. Family interviews intercut with glimpses of the patients' nursing home routine achieve a delicate balance, giving us, the viewers, access to the suffering and stress of family members without inviting a counterproductive drift into easy identification with them. Haneda elicits (and of course edits) testimony well-nigh devoid of emotional display. No family member loses control, discussing lives so sadly diminished by loss of control. Symptoms and difficult decisions are discussed with calm acceptance of unpleasant facts. A daughter-in-law faces the camera directly, describing in a matter-of-fact tone of voice Taka's increasingly odd behavior. The old lady's insatiable hunger led to frantic gobbling of entire pots of rice. She took to screaming out "Fire!" in the middle of the night. Tsue's son and daughter-in-law describe her habit of bundling up belongings and wandering off in search of her old home, a house long since demolished. Their faces in close-up betray no sign of emotion. They engage our thoughtful consideration of the problem at hand, not our sympathy with the pain its solution might have given them.

Haneda is equally careful not to explore the ramifications of senile debility in certain areas of family life, notably conflict. All manner of questions go unasked—questions as natural to cinema as they are to sociology. What conflicts developed in family relations as a result of eldercare? What role did the patient herself play—knowingly or unknowingly—in creating discord? How well did the family cope with the long-drawn-out demands on its resources of time, energy, and money? How was the decision made to surrender the patient to nursing home care? What were the emotional and financial consequences of that decision?

Needless to say, Haneda could count on her audience to be well aware of those and other real world parameters. Like the unhappy facts of incontinence, she could leave them to viewer discretion, as one might call the anxious gray area of personal consideration her film is apt to elicit in most of us. Audiences East and West might well differ with respect to another reason for Haneda's selectivity. The old-fashioned prohibition against washing your dirty linen in public was very much in force in 1980s Japan (as indeed it is today), whereas Americans at the time were learning to accept letting it all hang out as the norm for public discussion of any number of issues.

The World of the Senile is a story about women almost exclusively. Though men are statistically apt to be a nursing home minority East or West, Haneda all but ignores the handful of males the camera sees in passing. She does, however, pause to acknowledge an important gender difference in this twilight world of senile dependency. It arises out of her "dramatic" reliance on harmonious compassion as key to understanding the workings of this world. The camera comes to rest on an old man in a chair, alone in a corner in the right foreground. The narrator-director's voice-over explains that men tend to remain aloof. In the left background, women sit talking together. The next shot singles the old man out. He sits smoking, clearly quite indifferent to the contented gathering nearby. A similar situation occurs at the Christmas party. Old ladies in festive hats enjoy their sing-along. The old man sits glumly silent, hat askew, the picture of fuddled isolation.

No end of episodes counters that impression with one of suffering old women finding ways to bond in sympathy. Momoe and Taka are bonded that way. Taka's life of hardship as a poor widow worn down by caring for others comes to this oddly fitting end: it is now her turn to be looked after by a fellow senile sufferer. The camera closes in on Taka's usual manic monologue. A medium shot shows Momoe seated quietly alongside, settling the dishes neatly in front of her friend. Time and again the camera pauses to study this and other instances of supportive companionship. Preparations for the New Year holiday bring old ladies and staff together. Yae is seen stuffing a rice cake with bean jam. The camera takes notes of her dexterity; she is quite at home, her hands moving very fast, no sign of senility there. Yet we are quickly reminded of the larger sad reality. The director in voice-over compliments Yae. Yae smiles in close-up, admitting to a fact troubling to us but not to her: "I don't remember things like that. Something is wrong with my head."

The most heartwarming moment takes place away from the nursing home. All the patients spend New Year's holidays at home. Scenes of family intimacy are anticipated by a touching sample of meetings and greetings as relatives, some with children, come to the home to collect their kin. Two shots of the deserted nursing home introduce the most affecting scene. Sadako's family are seen at home in holiday attire, playing *hyakunin isshu* a *waka* poetry card game. A close-up shows Sadako's happy pride in knowing all the *waka* poems by heart, a matter of remembering verse in a 5–7–5–7–7 syllable pattern. As someone reads aloud the first two lines or even a single line of each poem, Sadako completes the rest without hesitation. Surely this old woman is fully alert. But of course she isn't "all there" at all. Asked her name, she says she doesn't know. She can't name family members either. She laughs in close-up, not at all embarrassed or upset. Her family, unfailingly kind as always, gives their names, knowing full well she won't remember.

Haneda's Stylistics of Sadness

No amount of "dramatic" selectivity can banish the sadness implicit in the subject of the film, yet Haneda is careful not to stray into bathos.

Tsue's search for her "lost" home is one example. Haneda dispenses with the usual pathetic assists—close-ups, dialogue, background music. Instead, she directs a noncommittal gaze on the facts of the matter. We turn from Tsue's bag lady wandering to a brief interview with her son and daughter-in-law. They explain that five times a day at least Tsue would bundle up clothes and set out on her quest.

Several shots of Tsue with her paper bag outside the nursing home show a male attendant tagging along. A series of long shots records their stroll through deserted countryside. A shot of Tsue alone comes to rest on her back. She becomes part and parcel of desolate surroundings. This moment says more about her desperation than any close-up of her face. They stop at a construction site to ask if anyone knows where Omachi is, Tsue's old home place. It's much too far to walk, yet Tsue insists that she must. The scene ends with a long shot of the attendant persuading her to try some other day. His patient kindliness speaks of a bond that goes some way towards curbing any sentimental tendency.

Related Haneda Films

Haneda's increasing concern over issues of eldercare was nurtured by professional and personal experience so it is no surprise that she scripted and directed three more films on the subject. In these, her thematic bias shifts to straightforward study of social groups as caregivers. The family's inability to care for its aged, especially those afflicted with senile dimentia, is taken for granted. Family matters are literally out of the picture here.

Anshin shite oiru tame ni [Aging Without Fear, 1990] is a case study of Ikeda, a small town in Aichi Prefecture. It marks a radical departure from the care depicted in *The World of the Senile*. Haneda introduces her audience to social welfare models in Denmark, Sweden, and Australia. All seek to accommodate the needs of senile eldercare, some by housing patients in group homes. Haneda's purpose is clear: to inspire her own countrymen to evolve a system "more flexible and humane" (Haneda 2002, 128).

Jūmin ga sentakushita machi no fukushi [A Town's Welfare System: The People's Choice, 1997] and its sequel, *Mondai wa kore kara desu* [The Problem Starts Now, 1999] picked up where Haneda left off in 1990. In this case, individual citizens of respond to issues and instances of eldercare, most notably a nursing care insurance scheme. Takasu in Akita Prefecture has a population of twenty-three thousand. It is large enough to pool significant resources yet small enough to elicit active participation in their allocation. The film celebrates the resulting achievement:

the town council's approval of a "Town Care" nursing facility built and maintained at public expense.

Most of Haneda's nineteen-year postretirement career was dedicated chiefly to films about the aged. She did take time out to make a monumental eight-hour documentary, yet it too had an end of life focus. Her subject was Kataoka Nizaemon, a Kabuki actor honored with "living national treasure" designation. Now in her seventies, she sees this most recent period of her work as vital, both for the role it may play in change for the better, and for her own understanding of herself as a "senior citizen" with a vested interest in knowing "what old age means."

Viewed in retrospect, her four films on care for the senile show Haneda somewhat ahead of the curve, willing to rethink and reconfigure a system of family eldercare deeply rooted in Japanese culture and tradition. *The World of the Senile* suggests that institutional care can make a success of the extended family model. Her later three films envision extending that measure of trust to groups as large as entire small towns.

Needless to say, no filmmaker is in a position to fast-forward any sector of public policy. (Here in fact I feel obliged to add a note of clarification based on personal experience, lest anyone imagine that Japan is adopting the eldercare models of any other country at any great rate. I regularly visit my own hometown of Nara where friends still talk of stiff resistance to any idea of committing senile family members to nursing home care. Perhaps this is to be expected in Japan's ancient capital, aware as its citizens tend to be of traditional ways and values, among them the Confucian virtue of filial piety, with all that means to propriety and self-sacrifice and where care of the family's elderly dependents is concerned.)

Significantly, Haneda's most recent documentary, *Owari yokereba subete yoshi* [All's Well That Ends Well, 2007], marks a radical departure from her previous works. It takes the viewer on a two-hour tour of end-of-life care for the aged. Haneda gives pride of place to the home care systems in Sweden and Australia, where doctors still make house calls. Her small camera crew of specialists is key to the success of visual witness that needs to be frankly inquisitive and at the same time compassionate and discreet. Though most of the footage is shot abroad, Haneda's purpose is to focus on what she sees as a crying need for reform in Japan. She takes special note of the sharp decrease in numbers of doctors willing to make house calls and invites the viewer to relate that shift to the fact that 80 percent of elderly Japanese now die in hospital. This is a documentary with a purpose. It affirms Haneda's conviction that the way forward must look back to the timeless tradition of respect and care for the aged. Her program notes for All's Well That Ends Well read like a manifesto: "Ideally, death should come as a final peaceful moment shared with close family members. We should ask what kind of system is needed in Japan in order to allow the elderly to die at home—a system that can allow us to uphold that basic respect for our common humanity" (Haneda 2006, 1).

Oriume (2002): A New Approach to Age-Old Family Drama

Matsui Hisako's debut film, *Yukie* links Japan and the United States in a refreshing new approach to issues raised by Alzheimer's. The film's special power derives from her decision to do what no director had done before: add the dimension of intercultural marriage to a study of an aged couple facing the complex process of loss that comes before death from this perverse disease.

Her second film, *Oriume*, is another Alzheimer's story, one that came to her attention through an accident of admiration. At a 1998 screening of *Yukie*, Matsui was approached by an old woman and her daughter who said they loved her film and wanted to give her a present. It was a manuscript account of the daughter's experience helping her mother cope with Alzheimer's.[7]

Matsui seized this opportunity to put women front and center in a family drama deeply rooted in Japanese culture. She, however, shifts the heroics to the distaff side. It is a strong, compassionate woman who takes charge as the challenge of Alzheimer's threatens to tear the family apart.[8] Gone are the melodramatic conventions of connubial romance at the center of *Yukie*. In their place Matsui puts a complex variation on that other classic drama of Japanese domestic life: mother-in-law and daughter-in-law conflict.

In *Oriume* a traditional source of conflict is reversed. Instead of a son's young wife brought into a household ruled by a tyrannical mother-in-law, we have an ailing, dependent mother-in-law coming to live with the wife of her son. The son is *not* the old woman's eldest, the usual natural successor to a husband as head of the family and as such his mother's designated champion. Here the old woman has elected to live with her third son. That docudramatic fact, by the way, runs counter to the view of many social scientists that parents still prefer to be dependents in the household of the eldest son.[9]

Matsui's film adaptation of one family's true story has an even more surprising twist: the mother-in-law's most steadfast ally and advocate is her daughter-in-law. The West has its tradition of conflict between the two, but in Japan the far greater likelihood of cohabitation gives that conflict a much larger (and more vexed) role to play in family history. The larger dramatic context of *Oriume* addresses a domestic issue of general concern East and West, namely, how the insidious and often slow deterioration that comes with Alzheimer's often threatens to destroy, not just the patient, but the caregiving family as well.

Opening Sequence

As the opening credits roll we meet two women in a scene that anticipates the tentative resolution we have yet to see them struggle to achieve. Masako and her daughter-in-law Tomoe are strolling in a park. They pass and greet a familiar sight, an old lady in a wheelchair pushed by a younger woman who appears to be her daughter-in-law. They come to a pond where Masako sets up to paint while Tomoe turns to reading. The camera takes notes of the way Tomoe looks over at her companion. Her expression in close-up speaks for the affection and compassion she feels for her mother-in-law. Another close-up studies Masako's peaceful and serene expression as she paints. The camera's inquisitive glances rouse our own curiosity. What story lies behind this harmonious relationship?

The title flashes on the screen. It speaks to the Japanese viewer in ways that must be explained in the West. *Oriume* translates as broken plum tree branch. Plum in bud or bloom would be understood. A branch of cherry would convey a different meaning, the traditional Buddhist awareness of the fleeting impermanence of all material things. In flower-aware Japan, *ume*, the plum, is known to be more enduring in bloom. The same is true of a branch of plum broken off and put in a vase. The title flashing on the screen connects that image with the old woman there. The Japanese viewer sees that this film has something to say about the energy and resilience of elderly people like this woman.

This opening sequence in Takahama anticipates the film's central issue: who will care for the elderly when they can no longer care for themselves? Unlike Haneda, whose story begins after the painful nursing home choice has been made, Matsui takes us back to a time when that fateful question still hangs in the balance. Her thematic thrust has to do with exploring the stages of a family's uncertainty leading up to the choice that will make such a difference in many lives, in this case, most especially the life of the daughter-in-law Tomoe.

Here at the beginning we see Masako herself witnessing the moment of awful truth she herself must face some day soon enough. She is bidding farewell to her old friend Tokiko. Tokiko sits in a wheelchair. The two old friends talk while a man stows Tokiko's luggage in a van. She is going to live with one of her sons. She advises Masako to do the same. Masako replies that her eldest son cannot accommodate her; and that going to live with the one who can, her third son, would be contrary to custom. The scene ends with a close-up of each woman's tearful face. Separation is clearly painful to both; both, we sense, are anxious about the future, each for her own sake and for her friend's sake.

Narrative Progression: Trial By Deterioration

A narrative eclipse of three months shows Masako exhibiting symptoms of Alzheimer's disease. The ensuing drama documents a familiar pattern as the stress of caregiving wreaks havoc on family life and leads to a last resort decision to institutionalize the sufferer. However, that decision in this case is reversed by the caregiver who has suffered most: daughter-in-law Tomoe. She is moved by compassion to undertake what seems impossible. The film records her struggle and eventual triumph in a context of widening involvement with family, friends, neighbors, and other Alzheimer sufferers.

The narrative moves from negatives as hateful as enmity and alienation to positives as loving as forgiveness and reconciliation. Masako and Tomoe become the protagonists. Together they define a new pattern, a place that family and community can reach by learning to take responsibility and share the burden of compassionate care. Yet this is no simplistic tale of triumph of duty over inclination. Matsui's film finds ways to plumb the hidden depths of an Alzheimer's victim's life, even as she herself loses touch with everyday surface reality. It is no slight on the director's achievement to call her film a docudrama. It has that carefully structured crescendo up to a midpoint turn from grief to a kind of joy. The themes worked out are familiar accordingly: suffering, struggle, confrontation, and conflict. Every family bond is put to the test by the stress of living with an old woman's loss of touch with herself, her family, and the world at large.

First Matsui offers an unsparing portrait of Alzheimer's dire progress. We see Masako presenting Tomoe with yet another pile of cleaning rags she has hemmed. The old woman's fixation on this busywork is destroying the family's supply of sheets. We see her shifting the garbage to the middle of the street. She washes the dishes with unnatural care. In a fit of irrational rage she throws things at Tomoe. As a source of discord, she is crude and cunning by turns, wolfing down food meant for the family and telling lies that pit one person against another.

The family's search for solutions grows increasingly desperate. Masako is shipped off to a daughter who returns her in short order. A nurse is tried but costs too much. The obvious worst solution—confinement to an institution—is prompted by Masako's increasing tendency to violence. Tomoe is the chief focus of her rage. At one point the old lady grabs her by the hair and drags her out of the house. Neighbors watch in horror as they struggle in the street. Masako also rages against herself. She takes up a kitchen knife and begs her son, Yūzō to stab her. Yūzō and Tomoe grow increasingly estranged. Finally, she storms out of the house and drives away, not knowing where to go. There is no choice left. Masako has to go.

This turning point midway through the film has a surprising outcome. As they drive Masako to the nursing home the old woman talks incessantly about her life. Childhood memories intersect with those of a widow struggling to raise a family alone and odd bizarre details of life with Yūzō's family. In actual fact she has lost control. Alzheimer's has muddled her sense of past and present reality. Yet this is a film, so it makes sense of an otherwise confused narration. We see clearly on screen what Tomoe has to imagine in response to the old woman's babbling. Matsui persuades us that Tomoe has a power of sympathy out of the ordinary. Why else would she respond so generously to this impossible old woman's tale of suffering hardship?

They go back home, all of them. Tomoe is determined to try one more time. From this point on, events take a more positive turn. Tomoe's heroic unselfishness leads to greater cooperation on the home front and greater ingenuity in seeking out help. Masako herself responds to compassion's many small inventions and to the sharing of problems and insights that come with contacts outside the family.

At a gathering of Alzheimer sufferers and their families, a facilitator elicits a breakthrough response from Masako. For the first time ever the old woman speaks clearly about her loss of memory and its affect on her behavior. She knows that she has wronged her daughter-in-law, although unwillingly; and that she is heartily sorry.

Another happy effect of outreach is the discovery of Masako's gift for painting. One of her paintings wins a prize at an exhibition. A dinner held to celebrate her prize affirms the familial and communal bonds that compassionate hard work has forged. Tomoe tells the good news to the neighbor whose hostility to Masako has yielded to sympathetic understanding of the suffering caused by Alzheimer's.

The film ends with a vignette similar to its opening. The family is visiting Masako's birthplace. They stroll through an orchard of plum trees in bloom. Tomoe listens attentively as Masako's ailing memory harkens back to the long lost past. The final shot frames two plum branches, one old and bent, the other young and straight, both in bloom. The image is comforting, though as we shall see, the ending of this film is anything routinely life-affirming.

Portrayal of Conflict Resolution

A director approaching a subject as rife with conflict and despair as Alzheimer's might be expected to create an atmosphere of mounting tension and sorrow as this irreversible disease debilitates its victim and damages caregivers, too. Matsui's film does go the despairing distance—up to a point. But then she breaks free of that darkly factual narrative. The mood of the film changes midway through, taking on a note of uplift as we see this human calamity eased somewhat by sympathy and understanding. Yet Matsui does something far more difficult than document the hopeful outcome of a single case history. She finds ways to take us into the mind of the patient of this bizarre disease.

The narrative matches the real-life drama of Masako's terrifying lapses into the raging confusion of senile dementia with sensitive recreations of the old woman's past-life memories. Matsui looks for ways to show us how the Alzheimer sufferer lives in a waking nightmare of conflicting realities. The latter half of the film is enriched with flashback visions of blissful childhood innocence shading into the darkness of memories long suppressed. Both extremes of the old woman's experience find expression as patient and family endure the harrowing progress of Masako's disease and discover the therapeutic value of knowledge and understanding.

The inspired camera work of Kawakami Kōichi lends a stylized clarity to scenes whose diagnostic value must be quickly understood as the narrative negotiates a number of difficult transitions between violent confrontation and quietly telling outcome.

Matsui makes good use of the simple long take to frame both extremes in this domestic drama. One long take of a minute and forty seconds shows us Mizuho, Tomoe's daughter, in her room. She is intent on fussing with her hair. Hearing her mother approach, she slips the small mirror in her hand into the desk drawer. Tomoe sits down nearby. She looks tearful, clearly in need of sympathy.

The camera's steady gaze observes this small crisis in relations. Tomoe's need is coldly met. Mizuho says bluntly that her mother invited Masako to join the family so that she herself could keep her part-time job. She adds that she thinks Tomoe hates her mother-in-law.

This confrontation meets its match in a later long take that follows the progress of Masako's most terrifying rage. The scene shifts quickly as the old woman drags Tomoe by the hair out into the street. The deep space defined by the camera's distant view of this harrowing incident creates an effect of studious detachment (or documentary objectivity). The street runs directly away from the camera so we see the struggle taking place in the foreground as neighbors gather in the middle distance. No one there makes a move. Help arrives from a distance. A young girl in school uniform comes running down the street. It is Mizuho. She lays hold of her grandmother gently and leads her into the house. A cut to the parents' bedroom shows Tomoe slumped across the bed. Mizuho enters and offers her mother the sympathy she withheld before. Tomoe clings to her daughter. This is the first time we see her weep.

The climactic reconciliation of mother-in-law and daughter-in-law takes place in a suitably symbolic heavy downpour. Yoshiyuki Kazuko brings long years of theatrical experience to her depiction of this most pitiful stage of Alzheimer's: the patient lost and wandering, a stranger to herself and all the world around. This powerful scene makes use of simple, striking contrasts. A series of long shots follows Masako along the waterfront of Nagoya Harbor. The mood of anxious urgency is underscored with sounds of heavy downpour mixed with music and a drum tattoo. Masako is dressed for dementia: skirt and jacket pulled on over nightgown.

A close-cut shot shows a frantic searching Tomoe riding a bicycle through the storm. The camera cuts back to Masako gazing at the ocean through the pouring rain. Close-up yields to flashback depicting Masako's disconnect—her vision of sea and shore bathed in sunlight of childhood memory. In the opening shot, a lovely woman is disclosed in a blue kimono carrying a parasol. She blends beautifully with sky and sea as several shots portray a loving mother and child relationship. Still, the camera keeps its distance. As the woman calls her name, the child Masako runs to her, exclaiming "Mother!" The mother, who has been away, embraces her, asking if she has been a good girl.

A cut back to the harbor shows Masako sopping wet in soaking rain, calling to her mother. We hear the rain beat harder as the camera cuts to what appears to be an office of some kind. Clearly, the old woman has been wandering some hours. A man comes out and tells her to wait inside. A close-up records her hopeless expression. The sound track drumbeat speaks for mounting tension broken by the sound of a car arriving. Masako beams. Her confusion yields to a shot clearly reminiscent of the mother/child bond of her flashback. Her greeting speaks for that ancient yearning: "How much I have longed to see you. . . ." Tomoe is cast in the light of surrogate mother.

The tension-harmony pattern returns a few scenes later as Masako learns that she will be taken to a nursing home. A number of close-ups register her reaction. One outsize look at her face shows an open book of sorrow and anger as she weeps. A reverse-field shot shows Tomoe and Yūzō facing Masako whose back is to the camera. Another close-up records the old woman's desperation. Seizing a kitchen knife, she asks her son to kill her.

The camera backs away enough to frame their struggle as Yūzō takes the knife away and embraces his mother. "Don't ever say that you want to die!" He cries. " I want to see you alive, no matter what!"

Here too, harmony is restored in terms relating to Masako's confusion of past and present. Consciously or unconsciously, Tomoe assumes the role of surrogate mother. She suggests that she and Masako sleep in the same room that night. A high-angle shot shows Masako on a western bed, Tomoe on a futon nearby. This studied focus lasts some forty seconds, drawing us into a complex world of growing sympathy. The action unfolding is simplicity itself; yet it unveils a complex relation between mother-in-law's senile retreat into the past and daughter-in-law's understanding of important truths lying hidden there.

For the moment, we see Masako's face in close-up as memory takes her back to the happiest time of her life, to her girlhood days as a seamstress in the Ginza. She croons a hit from the fifties, "Ginza Can-Can Girl," about a fashionable beauty enjoying herself in the heyday of that Tokyo hotspot. Returning to the present, after some hesitation, she asks Tomoe if they can share the futon on this, her last night in the house. A final medium shot shows them together there. Masako has fallen asleep. Tomoe wakes, sensing something strange. Lifting the coverlet, she finds Masako's hand on her breast. The soundtrack introduces a guitar motif used from this point on to speak for family solidarity. The inference here speaks for itself, especially in light of a childhood reminiscence shared earlier on. Masako's widowed mother had to leave her little girl to work away from home. That led to leaving altogether when the mother remarried. The following sequence depicts the turnaround trip to the nursing home. The atmosphere created could have been heavily despondent in tune with Masako's agony of separation anxiety. Yet Matsui relieves that tension with hopeful signs of growing intimacy between the two women. In fact, the sequence ends on a definite note of uplift as Tomoe comes to understand the nature of their bond.

But first must come the apparent sad necessity of taking Masako where she needs to go. Tomoe leads her to the car. Her own face tenses as Masako stiffens, grieved and unwilling. Yet the touching guitar motif from the bedroom scene returns, as if on purpose to correct our view of this as a moment of dreadful separation. That light touch is confirmed by the passing scene as the car makes its way along green suburban streets. We share the family's sense of welcome diversion from the stress and strain of recent unhappy events at home.

As they approach the famous Monkey Park, Masako is seized with a desire to revisit this scene of childhood delight. Tomoe agrees. Again, the simple device of flashbacks reinforces the theme, combining Masako's yearning for lost mother love with Tomoe's growing awareness of the old woman's plight.

The scene opens with several shots of Masako and Tomoe watching the monkeys. A medium shot—not once, but twice—singles out a mother cradling her baby. Masako is reminded of her own mother's way of holding her. A casual question from Tomoe effects the transition to Masako's past remembered. This flashback explains the film's title metaphor. We see mother and child on either side of an enormous vase. As the mother arranges branches of plum in bloom, she explains to little Masako: "The tree takes nourishment from its bark. Even if you break a branch and put it in the ground, it will take root and grow."

The sequence completes the allusion to Masako's enduring vitality, damaged as she is by her disease. She herself is consciously aware that the plum tree helps make sense of the beautiful strong mother she yearns for. She explains that the Chinese character for plum, *ume*, includes the radical signifying mother.

Another deft flashback conveys her sense of loss with powerful economy. A long shot returns to the child Masako playing alone on the beach, singing a children's song. The wistful guitar motif lingers in the background. A line-of-sight long shot follows a path leading up to a house in the distance. We have seen this place before, when the beautiful mother in a blue kimono hurried down to find her daughter on the beach. Now she is nowhere to be seen. The camera cuts back to the child playing and singing alone on the beach. This simple comparison works. We share the child's sense of forlorn abandonment.

We also share Tomoe's growing sense of Masako's inner life. Past and present converge in cinematic time as Masako's life unfolds through scraps of dialogue and flashbacks with the old woman's voice-over narration. It is a tale of loss and suffering too. The girl is beaten by her stepfather. She is widowed young, left alone to support four children. A number of shots take time to dwell on the faces of these women as Masako tells her story—a story of bitter experience her children have never heard. Tomoe's range of expression speaks for surprise, dismay, and the sadness of heartfelt sympathy.

The sequence ends with a distant view of a river. Buildings crowd the farther shore. Masako and Tomoe are on the nearer shore. They are tiny figures fading into the gloaming of a splendid evening. Could they still be on their way to the nursing home at this late hour? The wistful guitar we associate with their growing bond of tender understanding says quite clearly no.

Sure enough, a cut to Tomoe's kitchen finds them home as Yūzō returns from work, surprised to see his mother there. Several quick shots bring the narrative up to date. Tomoe smiles as she announces her decision to give home care another try. The family bond has gained in strength. Yūzō offers to help cook for the first time ever. Everyone lends a hand.

Coda: Harmony Restored

As mentioned before, the gathering Masako and Tomoe attend at the temple marks a turning point in the thematic progression of the film. This time their bond gains strength from a ray of hope offered all the assembled patients and families affected by Alzheimer's. One of the speakers makes two points which Tomoe takes especially to heart: "None of us can live without recognition; we all need to feel that others know who we are. . . . All those who come to this temple yearn for affection from their families."

The testimonial scene that follows is a trifle overdone. Encouraged to share her feelings, Masako describes the pain of memory loss, especially for one who was praised, even as a child, for having a retentive memory. As she speaks, the camera surveys the audience. Some are weeping openly. The appeal to tears grows stronger as Masako confesses to a contrarian tendency fostered by her confusion. She admits to being rude to her daughter-in-law when in fact she wants to express only thanks.

A close-up shows Tomoe's surprise. When Masako starts to weep, Tomoe takes a handkerchief from her purse and tosses it to her. Masako tosses it back. During this childish game, Masako's confession continues: "I would rather die than have Tomoe hate me. . . . I don't know why I am so cruel to her !" She ends with begging Tomoe's forgiveness. Everyone is in tears as the guitar motif returns with its bonding theme.

Mercifully, that larmoyant interlude yields to an upbeat focus on family solidarity and practical therapy. Masako takes up painting with notable success and domestic life makes room and time for the patient, inventive work of caring for her needs. A number of casual shots convey a sense that all may yet be well. As Tomoe hangs one of Masako's paintings, the camera glances at the book Yūzō is reading, a cookbook for men. In another scene, Mizuho is helping Tomoe hang laundry out to dry. Lest we miss the contrast to that earlier episode of mother/daughter confrontation, Mizuho now is heard to say that her mother has changed a lot. Tomoe answers by humming a tune. The alert viewer will recognize it as "Ginza Can-Can Girl," the song her mother-on-law sang that night they shared the futon.

From this point on, the film insists that its hope of positive outcome is real for each and every member of this family. That hope is expressed in an extended journey metaphor that leads us back to Masako's birthplace. This time the destination is for real, not a flashback figment of diseased imagination. We see the happy family in the car. Masako, too, is smiling. Here, too, the contrast with the earlier scene is obvious. Matsui is preparing her viewer, like this family, to "realize" the meaning of a place that speaks for Masako's deepest yearning.

An opening shot shows the pathway leading from the old house in the background down to the beach. The camera follows it now, not to find a lonely child, but tagging along behind a family in holiday mood. Yūzō and the children run ahead. A following shot shows Masako and Tomoe at a distance walking the beach. A medium shot closes in as Masako says how happy she is to return at last. This is the beach where she used to wait for her mother to come and visit her. She reminisces contentedly, then moves away from Tomoe. The camera follows. Masako journeys back in time, singing the children's song that marked her childhood waiting. What is she thinking beyond that reprise of memory? Presumably she knows that her life is winding down—but not alone, not now that her family understands this lifelong source of pain. Tomoe steps into the picture as if to confirm the point of the film, namely, that the bond between these women is firm and will hold through the difficult time ahead.

That message is reinforced by yet another pointed use of the title metaphor. The family's outing includes a visit to a forest of plums in bloom. Matsui takes full advantage of a scene astonishing in itself. An overhead pan surveys the blossoming loveliness. The musing guitar restates its theme. As the view shifts right, we see distant tiny figures wandering among the trees. The next shot singles out a huge old plum in bloom. A close-in cut reveals Tomoe inspecting its decaying bole. "It's hollowed out inside and still it blooms this beautifully," she says. "This tree is like my grandmother!" her son exclaims. Masako herself moves from tree to tree, savoring the blossoms. The camera follows, closing in once on her smiling face.

Matsui shies away from an ending quite that simple—simpleminded, some might say. *Oriume* ends on home ground, where battles with Alzheimer's are lost and won. We see Masako alone in her room. Her motions are unsettling to watch; those of a person not fully aware, not fully in control. The camera shifts to Tomoe in the living room. Masako comes in. Their conversation is peaceful and ordinary, yet sadly symptomatic. Masako doesn't know who Tomoe is. She thinks she is visiting strangers and is anxious not to outstay her welcome. She is ready to go home now, the home she left to move in with her son.

Next we see Masako and Tomoe seated across from one another at a table. Again, this could be an ordinary home event. But Tomoe is asking Masako where she lives. Masako gives her old address, the only one she remembers now. Tomoe is calm, an understanding, caregiving sharer now of the old woman's topsy-turvy world. They sip their tea and laugh together. This is the message Matsui is eager to convey. The instructor at the temple stated it clearly in that scene: "She wants to be accepted by those around her—accepted as she is. We social workers cannot take the place of family. All victims of Alzheimer's crave the family's affection."

The closing shot ends where the film began. This time it frames a painting of plum branches old and young, linked together, both in bloom. Still, the intelligence of this film persuades us of the need to feel uncertain too. After all, Masako still has the rest of her life to live. Her family has yet to endure that burden of care. Life can be long. Patience can run out. Matsui's documentary honesty throughout has presented hard evidence enough to suggest that Alzheimer's is a challenge first and last—with no cure more miraculous than the hard work of compassion.

Closure on Screen versus Real World Open Ending

Matsui's subtle message in the final sequence clearly echoes the altruistic message explicitly conveyed by the head of the nursing home in Haneda's *The World of the Senile*: "If you continue to nurse with respect for patients' feelings and thoughts, symptoms of senility can be lessened though not eradicated." One might say that Haneda and Matsui both subscribe to that philosophy, though their films approach it differently, thanks in part to genres as different as documentary and domestic drama.

Haneda's altruism looks beyond the family. Her point of departure lies beyond that traditional arena of confrontation and sometimes destructive refusal to look for outside help. Haneda's family of the 1980s has enlisted the aid of the larger context the director is at pains to show as capable of meeting the need. Her thematic thrust is faith in the social group as a benevolent extended family. As an actual system for delivering eldercare, it is new and forward-looking. Yet its view of life and social values is traditional as well, entirely consonant with Confucian ideals.

Matsui's family of the 1990s lives in a rapidly changing society, yet her presentation is equally consonant with tradition. She celebrates the time-honored bond between mother-in-law and daughter-in-law, and the paramount importance of family solidarity. She uses an actual family history to show how even a trial as severe as Alzheimer's care can lead to the kind of compassionate learning that strengthens its bonds.

In the realm of possibilities that opens up on screen, *The World of the Senile* and *Oriume* come together very nicely, imposing a sense of closure with emphasis on the virtues of compassion, filial piety, and duty exercised both by family and extended family. Off-screen, of course, the drama of actual real life is open-ended and apt to prove far less satisfactory. The range of possibilities there just naturally morphs in the direction of the problematic. Solutions may well not present themselves to problems as serious as a shortage of facilities designed to care for Alzheimer's patients and staff dedicated accordingly. A human interactions, too, are famously apt to prove unmanageable. What if the mother's deterioration in *Oriume* puts her beyond the reach of the daughter-in-law's devoted care? Caregivers, too, are entitled to survive. Yet what does entail in this tragic situation? And what of the viewer of films like these? It would seem that their makers invite us into a theater of the mind where a kind of courage is required, along with the intellectual and emotional growth real art inspires. In these two instances, that means accepting the paradox of endings that satisfy, even as they deny us any comfortable sense of closure.

Notes

The Agony of Eldercare

1. This figure—1.57 million—does not include young victims. See http://www.mhlw.go.jp/shingi/2004/06/s0621-5c.html.

2. There are about 4.5 million Americans with Alzheimer's. This number is estimated to reach 14 million by mid-century. See Gross, "Alzheimer's in the Living Room," 2004.

3. The film was shot during a two-month period from December 1982 to January 1983. Entitled *Chihōsei rōjin no kango* [How To Take Care of the Senile], it was originally intended as an educational film. After its completion, however, S. Haneda herself wanted to make it an independent film geared for the general public. Further editing and copyright permission from the patients' families took almost three years before a revised version was released with the new title *Chihōsei rōjin no kango* [The World of the Senile].

4. In this film, all the patients are victims of Alzheimer's or *chihō* (senile dementia), not of *boke* (dotage). Citing a number of Japanese scholars

like Hayakawa Kazuteru and Kikkawa Takehito, John Traphagan argues that while the *boke* condition is controllable and may be preventable, *chihō* and Alzeheimer's are associated with "a certain degree of fatalism." See Traphagan, *Taming Oblivion* (2000), 136.

5. The documentary defined by the World Union of Documentary was the type of work recording on film "any aspect of reality interpreted either by factual shooting or by sincere and justifiable reconstruction, so as to appeal either to reason or emotion, for the purpose of stimulating the desire for, and the widening of human knowledge and understanding, and of truthfully posing problems and their solutions." (Koningsbeg 1987, 88).

6. This documentary film was never issued as a video, due to strong opposition from the families that had been interviewed in it.

7. Matsui was so taken with it that she set right to work, scripting the story six times before she was satisfied. (The author's interview March 24, 2002).

8. She had this to say about her aim in *Oriume*:

> Senility is a hell for those who suffer from it and for those who look after them. It is what everybody thinks. Sometimes, however, strong women have means of finding a root of life, love, and joy when faced with hell. They move forward undaunted in the life they chose, bravely, without fuss. Understanding the pains of others, and the complexity of the world, they have the power to leap for the higher value as they endure the weight of their mission. I wanted to portray such strong women in ordinary homes, in ordinary life. I wanted my characters to show the truth that they can transform their unhappy fortunes to noble and joyous lives with their own power. (Matsui 1998)

9. Citing a number of interviews, a sociologist, Akiko Hashimoto claims that each Japanese person interviewed prefers co-residence with his/her oldest son. She also adds that "the unwillingness to leave matters undecided and the unwillingness to leave help up to voluntary goodwill" are the salient features of "the Japanese sense of security" associated with old age. See Hashimoto (2000, 21).

Lived Families

Chapter 5

Mass Arrests, Sensational Crimes, and Stranded Children

Three Crises for Japanese New Left Activists' Families

Patricia G. Steinhoff

The enduring image of family crisis in Japan is of intimate, face-to-face interaction that occurs inside the privacy of the home, with outsiders resolutely excluded. The real family crises I will discuss differ radically from this image and from whatever semblance of reality it may represent. These crises were set in motion by the political activism of a young family member whose initial conflict was not with the family at all, but with the Japanese state during the politically charged late 1960s. They became family *crises* when the student was arrested, but only some of them became family *conflicts*. Why did some become family conflicts, while others reinforced family ties?

Arrest situations require family members to deal with the crisis under completely different structural conditions from ordinary family interaction. The crises are characterized by separation, rather than close face-to-face interaction. The separation is spatial, with family members often in different geographic locations. It is also physical, with walls, partitions, and other physical barriers separating the family members even when they are in spatial proximity to one another. The separation is also temporal, with only intermittent, asynchronous communication taking place through the transfer of physical objects from one person to another through intermediaries.

Arrest crises are also fundamentally public, as opposed to the usual notion of the family as an intimate private space that is resolutely closed to outsiders. In these crises the state is a constant, physical presence, observing and manipulating the family's interaction for its own ends through the personnel of the criminal justice system. Equally important to my analysis is a fourth party that also intervenes and participates in the family crisis for its own ends: a support system that assists arrested New Left student activists. Since the support system is itself a part of the New Left, these family crises may also be understood as settings in which the larger conflict between the New Left and the state is played out.

This paper will examine three different types of arrest crises that Japanese activists and their families have faced, and the roles played by state actors and the New Left's support system as the crisis unfolds. The first type, the Mass Arrest Crisis, arose during the initial period of mass arrests at the end of the 1960s, when the greatest number of families faced their child's arrest for political activity and the New left's support system helped them deal with it. The second type, the Sensational Crime Crisis, arose when the activist child committed a serious, widely publicized crime, and the family faced both public censure and the child's grim future. The third type, the Stranded Child Crisis, arose when the arrest of an activist parent left a child stranded somewhere.

The data for this analysis derive from a long-term study of a relatively small number of Japanese radical activists from several interrelated armed clandestine groups, who have been the objects of intense Japanese police scrutiny for over thirty years. Through interviews, participant observation, and documentary materials, I have traced the roots of their activism back to the political and social context of the 1960s and followed their careers forward to the present. Much of my access to them has come about when they were arrested and entered the Japanese criminal justice system (Steinhoff 2003). Family conflict itself has not been central to my research, which focuses on the activists' confrontations with the state. Hence, this analysis centers on the kinds of family crises that arise as a direct result of my subjects' political activism.

The core of my sample consists of activists who first participated in the large public protest movements of the late 1960s in Japan along with many thousands of other students and ordinary citizens. Scholars who have studied the Japanese, German, Italian, and American protest cycles of this same time period of the late 1960s and early 1970s have found a very similar dynamic (Kriesi, Koopmans et al. 1992; della Porta 1995; Zwerman, Steinhoff et al. 2000). As protests escalated into violent confrontations with the police, the state initiated a severe crackdown using both normal legal means and extraordinary measures. Many people withdrew from protest activity as the risks of participation increased, but some became more radicalized by the repression and vowed to continue. When they could no longer protest openly, they went underground or into exile, where they engaged in more extreme covert activities and became much harder for the police to find. My colleagues and I have argued that these radical activists in armed clandestine groups should not be studied as an isolated phenomenon, but must be understood in the context of the broader protest movement from which they emerged (Zwerman, Steinhoff et al. 2000; Zwerman and Steinhoff 2005).

We also have learned from countless studies that social movement participants do not have distinctive psychological or individual characteristics that distinguish them from other people. Participation is largely a function of their social networks and structural availability. Within the broader social movement context, those who end up in the most extreme underground groups are products of the same contingent forces. They may have been radicalized by an early arrest or repressive confrontation, or they might have been available to go underground at a later point because they happened to avoid arrest earlier or entered the movement later. Consequently, it may be more productive to ask how people were eliminated from the original broad pool of protesters than to seek strong commonality among those who end up in extreme radical groups.

The Japanese case fits these general parameters well. At the peak of the Japanese protest cycle in late 1968 and early 1969, the state responded to the escalating violence of the protest movement with a heavy police crackdown that resulted in thousands of arrests, followed by prolonged detention and for many, indictment on criminal charges. New Left activists and their sympathizers responded to the mass arrests by participating in a loosely coordinated volunteer support system. Their aim was to sustain the protest movement by supporting students who were arrested for protest activities, and helping them carry their resistance into the criminal justice system.

Although many of my research subjects were not arrested in the Mass Arrest Crisis of the late 1960s, they were directly affected by it because they could no longer continue along the same path of public confrontations with the state. Instead, they either went underground or into exile in North Korea and the Middle East to continue their activity. Those who went underground were arrested in Japan in the 1970s and early 1980s and prosecuted for very serious crimes that resulted, directly or indirectly, from their resistance to the state. These arrests precipitated the Sensational Crime Crisis for numerous families. The exile groups in North Korea and the Middle East increased their numbers during the 1970s by bringing in more people through unorthodox means. They also began families of their own overseas. Since the late 1980s, many of the exiles have been arrested around the world, precipitating a second wave of criminal prosecutions of political activists in Japan that continues to the present. Other exiles and some of their family members remain overseas. The arrest of some exiles has led to the Stranded Child Crisis, in which the state and support organizations unexpectedly cooperated to help the families.

Each of the three crisis types affected families in a different way. After first establishing a baseline for the period prior to the first crisis, I will explore the propensity for family conflict in each type by examining both the general circumstances and some specific examples.

Activism and Family Conflict before the Mass Arrest Crisis

The historical experience of the cohort of Japanese young people who reached college age in the mid-1960s was distinctive in several ways. They were born in the immediate postwar years, when Japan was suffering from the devastation of war and poverty was the common experience of the great majority of families. As these children grew up, Japan's economy was recovering and moving into a long period of expansion that brought stability to family finances and a strong sense of optimism about the future.

The key to the future was education, and this generation was the first to experience the full effects of the Allied Occupation reforms in education and to reap their benefits. College education was extended to a broader proportion of this generation, but it still retained its aura as an elite achievement.

Consequently, any child who succeeded in getting into a university was already a success and a credit to the family. Within the parameters of their generation and its historical experience, university students had achieved a special status that conferred not only future rewards of economic security, social status, and leadership, but also the immediate privilege of freedom to spend their time as they wished, with minimal social, academic, and economic responsibilities. Parents, universities, students, and much of the society as a whole concurred in this view of their status. This shared perception, in turn, provided a strong foundation for positive parent-child relations. These were good kids who had fulfilled parental expectations; there was no fundamental structural basis for family conflict in their relationship.

The massive 1960 protests against revision of the Joint Japan-US Security Treaty (Anpo) helped to normalize participation in mild political protest activity such as street demonstrations as an acceptable activity for citizens and students (Sasaki-Uemura 2001). The 1960 Ampo protests also provided a bridge to the protest issues of the late 1960s, many of which were also related to the terms of the Japan-US Joint Security Treaty and its next scheduled revision in 1970. After a lull of a few years in the early 1960s, participation in protest events again became quite a routine part of student life as this generation was entering universities. The large urban areas where most college students were concentrated provided good conditions for mobilization, especially for students living away from home.

By 1967, when Vietnam War-related activity began to impinge upon U.S. bases in Japan and opposition to Japan's support of the U.S. position grew, there were multiple, nationally organized student organizations ("sects") in fluid coalitions or in competition with each other. They sometimes participated in larger demonstrations organized by other political or citizens' organizations, and at other times organized their own protests. Unaffiliated or "non-sect" students also joined the protests regularly. Following the 1960 Ampo protests, the police had steadily increased their manpower, equipment, and training for riot control. Some of the "sects" began to use more provocative tactics against the well-fortified riot police lines deployed at protest demonstrations. As the level and severity of protests rose, the police themselves became the symbolic target representing the state's repression of its citizens.

Japanese society in general was quite divided about the issues of protest in the late 1960s. Much of the public opposed the government position on many of the key issues, as did the major *Asahi* and *Mainichi* newspapers. Parents who belonged to blue or white collar unions often participated in mild protest demonstrations or at least voiced considerable sympathy for the opposition point of view. For many parents, the behavior of the riot police brought back unpleasant memories of overbearing political and military police in prewar and wartime Japan. When there was some sympathy about the issues and protest was a relatively low-risk activity, it was not a great source of family conflict.

Parents whose children were away at big city universities would really only learn about their involvement in protest if the student happened to be injured or arrested. Even then, they might not find out if the injuries were not serious. Arrests of students for protest activity in the mid-1960s were also rather minor matters. The arrests were for misdemeanor offenses and the standard procedure was for the student to apologize and be released after a short time. If a guarantor was required, the student was just as likely to call a professor as a parent. Police, professors, and parents regarded such arrests as youthful indulgences of no great consequence, while the students saw them as a temporary inconvenience or perhaps a badge of honor.

Among students who either lived at home or were in frequent contact with their parents, the limited evidence we have suggests a rather universal parent-child dynamic, with some characteristic Japanese nuances. Family members avoided much potential conflict by mechanisms such as maintaining physical distance, withholding information, and limiting verbal interaction. Moreover, in many families there was no conflict either because of the parents' political and emotional sympathies, or because a loving and supportive mother offered unconditional acceptance without paying much attention to the specific details of the child's activity (Pharr 1981).

Shigenobu Fusako's description of how her parents reacted to her arrest in 1970 illustrates this pattern. Already a prominent Red Army Faction activist, Shigenobu was living with her parents and sister in a Tokyo suburb and was under constant police surveillance. She had left the house wearing her sister's clothes as a simple disguise. At the bus stop a short distance away, two plainclothes policemen confronted her and asked which sister she was. Not wanting to cause trouble for her sister if she happened to come out of the house, Shigenobu admitted who she was. The police had a warrant for her arrest, but she persuaded them to let her go back home and return her sister's clothes before she went to the police station. The officers went back to the house with her and waited outside while she changed clothes, explained the situation to her sister, and packed the personal items she would need in jail. Just then her father returned home. Shigenobu told him it looked like she was getting arrested again and her father, who had participated in a right wing coup attempt against the government in the 1930s, replied, "Well, hang tough. Don't worry about anything at home."

A police car had pulled up in front of the house, attracting the attention of the neighbors, who were also supportive. She waved to them as she went off in the police car. Later, when her mother came to visit her in jail, she recounted how at the train station on the way to the jail she had passed some students collecting signatures on a petition. For the first time in her life, she suddenly decided to sign it. When she did so, the students recognized the name Shigenobu and asked her to convey their greetings to her daughter. Her mother reported that the students seemed really excited about meeting Shigenobu Fusako's mother, but the mother couldn't remember what their petition had been about. Although Shigenobu's arrest came somewhat later in the protest cycle, the family interaction reflects the attitude of urban parents who supported their child's activism even if they did not agree with her ideas or even comprehend them (Shigenobu 2005).

The Tug-of-War Over Families in the Mass Arrest Crisis

By the fall of 1968, circumstances had changed considerably as the protest cycle neared its peak. Although there were still massive street demonstrations protesting a variety of loosely related issues, they often culminated in violent clashes between radical students and riot police that caused heavy injuries on both sides, as well as extensive property damage. Student protest was becoming a much higher risk activity. Arrests were now frequent and indiscriminate, as police desperately tried to restore order on the streets during major protest events. In addition, campus protests were spreading like wildfire, with students occupying campus buildings for extended periods, and paralyzing normal academic life. Although the public still strongly backed the protesters on the core issues, there was less and less support for violent protest tactics.

With arrests at violent street demonstrations rising and riot police being called in to end campus building occupations, the police quietly implemented a new policy. They began to hold arrested students in police jails indefinitely and sought to prosecute them, rather than quickly releasing the students back to the streets. They also began serving arrest warrants for more serious charges of conspiracy or inciting to riot, to deter student leaders who may not even have been present when a demonstration turned violent. In response, supporters of the New Left expanded and adapted existing volunteer legal support activities, loosely coordinating them through a new clearing house organization called "Kyūen Renraku Sentā" (Relief Contact Center, nicknamed Kyūen). Their goal was not only to assist arrested students, but also to deal with the crisis in ways that would help sustain the momentum of the protests and encourage continuing resistance. The number of volunteer support groups working with Kyūen proliferated rapidly in 1969 and 1970 as the Mass Arrest Crisis grew (Steinhoff 1999).

Since arrested students could no longer expect to be released quickly with minimal consequences and return to the streets for further protest, they could either acquiesce to police pressure to give up their protest activity, or continue their resistance through the criminal justice system. The Kyūen system supported the latter alternative by utilizing the new civil liberties protections in the postwar constitution. These included: constitutional protection for freedom of speech, political organization, and assembly; the right to remain silent when questioned by police and prosecutors; the right to be represented by a lawyer; and the right to a public trial.

The starting point was a twenty-four hour telephone hotline maintained by Kyūen volunteers, with a number that has been memorized by generations of students as GO-KU IRI, I-MI Ō-I (Going to jail has great meaning), or 591–1301. A massive education campaign taught students their right to remain silent, their right to be represented by a lawyer, and the magic number to call. When students were arrested and chose to use this support system, they would refuse to give any information, even their names, would ask to speak to a lawyer, and would give the Kyūen hotline number for their one permitted telephone call.

Police tried to get the students to talk and strongly tried to dissuade them from using a lawyer, but ultimately they were legally required to permit access to a lawyer. The arrestees were not allowed to make the call themselves, so the police were obliged to call the hotline to report the student's request for a Kyūen lawyer. Since the students were refusing to talk, Kyūen initially knew them only by their booking number at a particular police station. Kyūen then dispatched a lawyer to interview the student at the police station, reinforce the importance of refusing to talk, and arrange to address the student's most urgent needs. After major demonstrations in Tokyo at which there were hundreds of arrests, Kyūen's small band of volunteer lawyers was stretched thin interviewing arrested students at police stations all over the city. Many students had not yet met with a lawyer after three days in the police jails, when they were brought to court for mandatory arraignment in order to justify continued detention, so Kyūen lawyers sometimes set up tables at the court to interview them.

The strategy of the police was to try to get personal information from the students so they could search their living quarters, track down their associates, and enlist the cooperation of their parents in pressuring the students to leave the movement. It was basically the same strategy the prewar Tokkō (Special Higher Thought Police) had used against the underground Communist movement in the 1920s and 1930s, which culminated in the mass movement of *tenkō*, or renunciation of an antistate political commitment while under pressure (Steinhoff 1988; Steinhoff 1991). The New Left students of the late 1960s and their supporters not only understood the state's strategy in precisely those terms, but also had stronger weapons against it in the postwar Constitution. To this day, New Left activists who use the Kyūen strategy to resist the state after being arrested are reported to be "Kanzen mokuhi, hi-tenkō de tatakainuite-imasu." (fighting to the end by maintaining silence and refusing to *tenkō*).

In a direct carryover from prewar practices, the *tenkō* strategy of the police relied heavily upon the use of family ties and emotional bonds to get the political offender to renounce a political commitment and return to ordinary, nonpolitical life (Steinhoff 1991). Consequently, the Kyūen resistance strategy also tried to enlist the support of parents. To do this effectively, they had to get to the parents before the police did, and make themselves the conduit for the parents' interaction with their arrested child. They could only do this if the arrested student was maintaining silence and the police had not yet learned the student's name and address.

In addition to checking whether the student had any injuries or other immediate problems, the Kyūen lawyer doing the initial interview would learn the student's name, current address, and student movement affiliation, and would also ask the student's permission to contact his or her parents. This information, on hundreds of students arrested and interviewed in the aftermath of a big protest demonstration, or on individuals arrested one by one on warrants, was brought back to the Kyūen office, where volunteers began contacting the friends and families of the arrestees. The basic message to both was the same: do not try to contact the arrestee directly, because you will be playing into the hands of the police and will hurt both the arrested person and other people. Instead, do as the student wishes and work through Kyūen.

In the early period, when students were arrested indiscriminately at demonstrations, Kyūen's approach to parents was to begin by explaining that although the student had been arrested, their child had not done anything wrong and wanted to fight against this injustice. The arrested child had called Kyūen and asked for their help, and now Kyūen was there to help the parent help the child. In the widely distributed pamphlet *Kyūen nōto* (1969), they urged parents to remain calm and follow the course that Kyūen had laid out. Students who lived at home often left a copy of *Kyūen nōto* on their desk when they went out to a demonstration, so their parents would find it and learn what to do if the student was arrested.

Kyūen's first task was to keep the parent from going to the police and inadvertently telling them things that would undercut the arrestee's stance of resistance. Later editions of the pamphlet reveal how parents were likely to respond to the arrest crisis and how Kyūen tried to prevent this.

> There are mothers who want to know as quickly as possible at what police station their child is being held, who take the child's picture around to all the police stations looking for him, and parents who go immediately to take things to their child and jabber to the police. How delighted the police are to receive them. And then there are family members who bow lower and lower, apologizing to the police.
>
> While the arrested person is diligently maintaining his silence, they blab to the police his name and school, workplace, and everything else.... This causes all sorts of trouble for the arrested person in the interrogation.
>
> .... maintaining silence is the strongest weapon the arrested person has. If that weapon gets snatched away by the parent, and what you thought was going to help the arrested person

has the opposite result, won't that be a very unfortunate thing for the family? (Kyūen Renraku Sentā 1977, 86–87)

To counter the parent's natural instincts, Kyūen urged them to respect the choice their child had made to follow the Kyūen strategy of resistance.

> In the secret depths of their hearts, from the love of their own flesh and blood, the parents want to stand face to face with their arrested child as soon as possible. If they oppose the arrested person's ideas and actions, it is fine that they want to clearly express their opposition, but if they also respect the arrested person's feelings and want to understand his position and support it, they should follow Kyūen's directions. (Kyūen Renraku Sentā 1977, 86)

A subsequent revision of the pamphlet reminded parents even more bluntly of why they needed to respect their child's wishes.

> Whether you are opposed to the arrested person's ideas and actions or support them, while the person is in the custody of the authorities, he is in a special condition in which you cannot have a free conversation with him, so first of all you must respect the arrested person's wishes. (Kyūen Renraku Sentā, 1978, 123)

As these messages make clear, Kyūen faced a formidable task in keeping parents from rushing to the police station to find and help their children.

If the police got to the parents first, there was little Kyūen could do. However, even if the parents managed to get their child out of jail, if the child went back to school away from home, there was no guarantee that he or she would actually leave the movement, as the case of the late Himori Kōyū demonstrates. Himori was a freshman at Ritsumeikan University in Kyoto, from the northern prefecture of Akita. In January 1969, he joined students from all over Japan and went to Tokyo to support the Tokyo University conflict. He was arrested in a building on the campus and charged with preparing weapons. Two weeks later Himori's mother received a call from the Akabane police station in Tokyo and learned that her son was not in Kyoto, but in the Akabane police jail in Tokyo. She immediately rushed to Tokyo, where she enlisted the help of several friends and in her view, caused a lot of trouble for them. She reports, "I cried and cried, wondering what kind of a star I was born under." (Himori 2005) It is not clear how much effect his mother's intervention had on his case, but he was released from jail. Himori went back to Kyoto, where he gained new stature among his classmates because he had been arrested in the Tokyo University conflict. In June, he was convicted and received a one year suspended sentence. He went on to devote the rest of his life to the movement, maintaining very limited contact with his family.

Initially, Kyūen had considerable success in promoting the strategy of resistance within the criminal justice system. Because most of these arrests took place during or right after large demonstrations or campus conflicts, and clearly represented a change in police tactics, if Kyūen could reach the parents first, it was relatively easy to persuade them that their child had done nothing wrong. Since Kyūen was contacting the parent at the child's request, they also had reasonable success in getting parents to channel their contacts with the child through Kyūen instead of going directly to the police. As letters from parents published in the Kyūen newspaper reveal, even some parents who had initial contact with the police later worked through Kyūen Renraku Sentā to support their child's resistance (Kyūen Sentā #8 (12/10/1969), and #9 (1/10/1970), reprinted in Kyūen Shukusatsuban Kankō Iinkai 1977).

To handle the distribution of aid such as food, clothing, and personal supplies to arrested students while preventing direct contact by parents and friends, Kyūen arranged a massive relief effort based on geographic assignment of volunteers to neighboring police stations. Labor unions, student organizations, women's groups, and ordinary housewives—including the mothers of arrestees—collected clothing and supplies for emergency packets, and made rice balls and sandwiches to feed the prisoners. They delivered their relief supplies to a particular police station to be given as "sashiire" to unnamed prisoners with specific booking numbers. In this way, volunteers could feel they were helping the people they cared about while supporting their efforts to maintain silence. Parents could also send parcels of clothing and other supplies directly to the Kyūen office, with all personal markings removed. The volunteer staff then delivered the student's own overcoat, blanket, and other items to the police station jail and sent them in using the student's booking number.

In postwar Japan, there is no right to have counsel present during interrogation, and even students represented by counsel are allowed to speak to their lawyers for only 15–30 minutes once or twice a week. The rest of the time, including 10–12 hours of interrogation per day, the suspect has to hold his own with the police. When not being interrogated, the suspect is under continuous surveillance in a cage-like police station cell, with every detail of his eating, sleeping, bowel habits and demeanor reported to the interrogators. Kyūen believed that the suspect's strongest defense was to concentrate on refusing to talk.

Detailed accounts of such interrogations of arrested students reveal that the strategy is to break down the suspect's defenses psychologically by invoking the themes of parental suffering, abandonment and treachery by peers, and the unscrupulous motives of political defense lawyers. At the same time, the police encourage the suspect to regard at least one of the interrogators as a kindly paternal figure (Takikawa 1973; Takazawa 1983; Tokyo San Bengoshikai Gōdō Daiyō Kangoku Chōsa Iinkai 1984; Kataoka 1985; Arai 1986; Sato 1989; Maruoka 1990). Young political activists had prepared themselves to keep silent despite mean, rough treatment by interrogators. They often had fewer defenses against paternalism. And unless they happened to have radical parents, they were particularly vulnerable to the repeated suggestion that their behavior had brought terrible shame and hardship to their families (Takazawa 1983; Kataoka 1985; Arai 1986).

Japanese prosecutors tend not to pursue cases that they are not certain of winning (Johnson 2002). There is a big gap between the arrest and indictment figures for students during this period, but it is impossible to determine whether students avoided indictment by keeping silent until police decided they did not have enough evidence to indict, or if the students succumbed to interrogation pressures and agreed to go home and behave themselves—with or without help from a pleading parent. What is clear is that from the point of view of the parent, the Kyūen strategy was a hard, counterintuitive choice that was probably far easier to make if the parent lived far away.

If the student was indicted, the next step in the New Left strategy was to mount a full trial. The overwhelming majority of criminal indictments in Japan are preceded by a confession and followed quickly by the defendant's acceptance of the prosecution's statement of the facts of the case, which is the equivalent of pleading guilty. In a single hearing a judge hears the prosecutor's charge and the defendant's acceptance, usually accompanied by some statement of contrition or apology, and then sets a relatively light sentence. Well over 90 percent of all criminal cases are processed in this way (Castberg 1990).

By contrast, the Kyūen strategy was to refuse to accept the prosecution's statement of the case, in effect pleading not guilty to the charges and opting instead for a full trial before a three-judge panel. Such a trial was usually only possible if they used a lawyer provided by Kyūen Renraku Sentā, since most privately retained lawyers would automatically counsel their clients to plead guilty and use contrition to try to get a more lenient sentence from the judge. A full trial would necessarily take a lot longer, especially since Japanese trials do not run continuously, but instead meet for one or two half-day sessions a month over an extended period of time.

The full trial offered only a very small probability that the defendant would be found not guilty, but that was not its primary purpose. Rather, a full trial would tie up state resources, require the state to justify its indictment by producing evidence (which in the absence of a confession would be considerably more difficult), and would offer the defendant a public forum in which to explain his political motives. The trial itself was a legal entitlement for a person charged with an ordinary criminal offense; what made it a political trial was the motivation behind the demand for a full trial and the legal strategy of the defense. To reinforce the political message and also to maximize their thinly stretched legal resources, the Kyūen lawyers tried to get students who had been arrested as part of the same protest event tried together, so they could give a political rationale for their actions. The judges and prosecutors, on the other hand, preferred to try each person individually on the specific criminal charges.

Whenever possible, the defense took the position that their clients were engaging in the constitutionally protected exercise of free speech and assembly, and that the charges against them violated the Constitution. Although they were unlikely to prevail in such claims, in fact there were many issues that the courts had not yet fully decided. Beyond whatever legal arguments the defense posed, however, Japanese trials provide several opportunities for the defendants to make their own statement to the court. The student defendants used those occasions to explain their political philosophy and emphasize the political basis for their actions. They were simultaneously supporting the defense lawyers' legal arguments and using the court as a public forum to present their views. They were also carrying on a long tradition in the Japanese Left of using trials as political forums and rallying points (Mitchell 1992).

At the trial stage, then, a student wanting to follow the Kyūen strategy would opt for a full trial using Kyūen lawyers, and would seek a group trial if possible. In the first few years of these procedures, student defendants were generally released from custody after indictment or shortly after the trial began. Even so, the Kyūen strategy unquestionably would prolong the trial period and probably would result in a more severe sentence, which might in turn damage the child's future employment prospects. Parents who consulted a private lawyer would generally have been advised not to follow the Kyūen strategy. It was thus even more counterintuitive for a parent to accept the strategy at the trial stage, especially if they could afford to hire a private lawyer.

Family pressure probably led many more students to drop out of the movement at this point. Even though the child complied with the parents' demands, the result often left the child with a residual sense of weakness for having cooperated with the police, alienation and shame at abandoning and perhaps even harming his friends, and resentment against parents who had used their own weapons of guilt to pressure the child into compliance. The parents who insisted on their way of dealing with the Mass Arrest Crisis as opposed to the child's preference were setting the stage for future family conflict. Like much interpersonal conflict in Japan this might not be expressed openly to family members, but would instead be characterized by withdrawal, behavior changes, and much silent suffering. One of Kyūen's ploys was to raise the spectre of these potential consequences to parents early on. This was a powerful threat for mothers whose primary child rearing strategy was to maintain a close, positive emotional bond of *amae* with the child.

Despite the counterpressures, substantial numbers of students did use Kyūen lawyers and mount full political trials in the 1969–1972 period. Many of these were group trials for defendants from a particular university conflict. In order to provide support for the defendants and paralegal assistance to the lawyers, a support group was organized for each separate trial, composed of friends and associates of the defendants and other people who supported the New Left cause. Trial support group members attended trial sessions, received briefings from the lawyers after the sessions, and often met on other occasions to socialize and perform various services connected with the trial. If any of the defendants were still being held in unconvicted detention, the support group also provided extensive personal support to them (Steinhoff 1999). Parents were encouraged to participate in the support groups and in some cases had their own parents' group.

Of the nearly one thousand students who were arrested during the Tokyo University conflict in January 1969, 769 were held the full twenty-three days, after which 509 of them were formally charged in an unprecedented mass indictment. Most were still in custody two months later (Gōdō kyūen nyūsu #3 (4/25/1969):3; reprinted in Kyūen Shukusatsuban Kankō Iinkai 1977). In addition to various support groups already established for different subgroups and sect affiliations among these arrestees, one hundred of their parents from all over the country organized a separate family support group called Tōdai Sō Giseisha o Mamoru Kazoku no Kai [Parent's Association to Protect the Tōdai Struggle Victims] on March 30, 1969 (Kyūen Sentā Sōkangō, 4/25/1969:2; reprinted in Kyūen Shukusatsuban Kankō Iinkai 1977). The use of the term "victims" (*giseisha*) for the arrested students underscores the position that the students were innocent and the authorities were at fault. By September, 415 of the 509 Todai defendants were still pursuing the joint trial strategy, 60 percent of whom were still in police custody after seven months (Kyūen Sentā #5, 9/10/1969:4; reprinted in Kyūen Shukusatsuban Kankō Iinkai 1977).

Subsequently, parents groups formed after mass arrests at each major demonstration. Seventy families of students arrested in the May 1969 ASPAC demonstrations quickly formed a parents group (Kyūen Sentā #3, 6/25/1969:2; reprinted in Kyūen Shukusatsuban Kankō Iinkai 1977). Many high school and even junior high school students, most of them still living at home, participated in the ASPAC demonstrations and were arrested. They, too, were following the Kyūen procedures and refusing to talk to the police, but minors under the age of eighteen were supposed to be handled through family court and the juvenile protection system. If a Kyūen lawyer discovered that the arrestee was a minor, the advice was to tell the police his or her age, but not name. This would immediately get the minor transferred out of the police station to a juvenile facility, where interrogation methods would not be nearly as harsh. In November, the parents group for students arrested in the big October 21 Anti-War Day protests reported that of the 1,270 young people arrested, virtually all of those held for the initial three days were steadfastly refusing to talk, even though many of them were minors (Kyūen Sentā #7, 11/10/1969:5; reprinted in Kyūen Shukusatsuban Kankō Iinkai 1977).

Kyūen Renraku Sentā set up its own central Kazoku no Kai, composed of dedicated parent volunteers who sent representatives to help organize the family members in other support groups that formed after specific waves of mass arrests. With the aid of these experienced and dedicated members, the new trial support groups became powerful socializing agents for parents. I observed this process of parent-to-parent socialization two decades later, when I was following the trial of Shibata Yasuhiro, the first of the Red Army hijackers living in exile in North Korea to be arrested and tried in Japan. This trial occurred in 1990, but the charges stemmed from Shibata's actions during the Mass Arrest Crisis period, and the dynamics of support group interaction with the parent were similar.

The defendant's father had come up from Kansai to testify about his son's early life. After his testimony, obviously ill at ease, he sat in the visitors section of the courtroom next to the mother of someone in the same exile group. During a break in the trial proceedings another activist's father, who participated regularly in Kyūen support groups, took the defendant's father in hand, introduced him to other support group members, and talked to him through the break. Later he commented that the defendant's father was more relaxed after they had talked. He said that new parents always feel terribly isolated and think they cannot communicate with anyone. They are always greatly relieved when they meet others who have faced the same situation (field notes, July 12, 1990 Shibata trial session, Tokyo District Court).

Although the defendant's father was quite politically conservative and was initially uncomfortable around the support group members, they quickly won him over with their kindness and friendly acceptance. At subsequent trial sessions, he was greeted warmly, fussed over, and encouraged to participate in support group activities. As the trial ended, the support group discussions turned to whether the defendant should appeal or just begin serving his relatively short sentence. The father was encouraged to offer his opinion, which was that the son should come home as soon as possible and behave like an adult by marrying and having a family. The support group members listened politely, but emphasized that everyone had to respect and support the defendant's own decision. The support group members disagreed with the views that the defendant's father expressed, but were unfailingly gentle and polite in talking with him (field notes 9/28/1990, 10/30/1990, 12/20/1990, 5/11, 1991 from Shibata trial sessions and support group meetings).

In summary, in the Mass Arrest Crisis a high proportion of the students arrested chose to follow the New Left strategy of resistance promoted by the Kyūen volunteer support system. Parents were faced with the hard choice of cooperating with the police in pressuring their children to leave the movement, or supporting the child's desire to continue resistance in the criminal justice system. The latter choice would not only keep the child entangled in the criminal justice system far longer, but could have damaging consequences for his future employment. Parents who cooperated with the police and pressured the child to leave the movement generally succeeded, but left the child with feelings of guilt and resentment that could do long-term damage to family relations.

What determined the parent's choice? Some of it undoubtedly stemmed from the parent's own sympathies with the issues about which students were protesting, since students with liberal parents were more likely to be inclined to participate in protest in the first place. However, a major factor at the peak of the protests, when huge numbers of students were swept up in street or campus demonstrations, was simply whether the student used the Kyūen strategy of maintaining silence after arrest and had requested a Kyūen lawyer. This allowed Kyūen the opportunity to reach the parent before the police had identified the student and contacted the parents, and gave Kyūen the chance to try to persuade the parent to do as the student wished because the student had not done anything wrong. The parent still had to decide what to do, and of course many other variables entered into that decision.

Parents in remote and more conservative parts of Japan were much more vulnerable than urban parents to community disapproval, and thus were more likely to view their child's arrest as a calamitous disgrace to the family. The mother rushing to Tokyo to extricate her child from jail was concerned about both the child's well-being and the whole family's reputation, which the child had damaged. And while the police were telling the child how badly he had hurt his family, at the same time they were exacerbating the injury by publicly hounding the family. Police and parents together used traditional weapons of guilt and shame to redirect the child to their aims.

By contrast, parents who cooperated with their child's desire to follow the resistance strategy became closer to the child through the process, and also received emotional support from other parents in the same situation. In the long run, the majority of the students who followed the resistance strategy also ended up leaving the movement when their sentences were completed, because by that time the protest cycle was waning and there were fewer opportunities to rejoin the movement. The state's repressive mass arrest policy did succeed in breaking the back of the protest movement, but it left behind a corps of more dedicated and radicalized participants who continued to protest through underground movements or exile groups. The dynamics of family conflict during the Mass Arrest Conflict indirectly created a greater likelihood of family support and a much lower probability of family conflict for those who remained active after this period. Nonetheless, some remained active in later years by cutting ties to their family, either because of prior family conflict, or because their underground activity demanded complete separation from family for their mutual protection.

The Shock of the Sensational Crime Crisis for Families

Unlike the mass arrest crisis, in which criminal charges were relatively light and family members could easily be persuaded that the child had not really done anything wrong, Sensational Crime Crises unfolded in the harsh glare of media publicity that focused directly on the family's responsibility for whatever the child was accused of doing. The sensational acts first appeared to the public as front page news. They were presented as political or "crazy" acts perpetrated by Japanese radical activists whose identity was not yet known, although in many cases some organization took responsibility with a public message. Initially, family members shared the public's horror at the act and sympathized with its victims. Subsequently, they learned that their own child had been arrested as one of the perpetrators. This crisis proved particularly difficult for families to handle, and sometimes resulted in tragedy.

Parents facing a Spectacular Crime Crisis might be confronted with substantial evidence that their child had indeed done something terribly wrong, but even in these cases there was often an equally good basis for questioning police behavior or the validity of the charges. Although activists who write about arrests in the *Kyūen* newspaper are quick to claim "detchi-age" or frameup, Kyūen Renraku Sentā has in fact been involved in a number of serious cases where police and prosecutors doggedly pursued charges against innocent people (Kyūen Renraku Sentā 1973; Takazawa 1983). It is particularly difficult to fight such charges when the crime has been sensationalized in the media and police are under heavy pressure to solve it. Whether the parents believed the child was innocent or guilty, they still wanted to help and protect their child out of unconditional parental love. Often in Sensational Crime Crises the charges were serious and the defendant faced the likelihood of long incarceration or even the death penalty. Under these circumstances, the Kyūen strategy of demanding a full trial and prolonging the trial period further through appeals of the convictions made much more sense.

A New Left activist arrested for a sensational crime was highly unlikely to be released on bail at any time during the legal proceedings. He or she would routinely be held long beyond the normal twenty-three day period for interrogation by police and prosecutors through the device of rearrest on a different charge. After indictment, the defendant would be held in unconvicted detention on the grounds that he or she might destroy evidence if released. Even though this reason vanishes after the prosecution has completed the presentation of its case, typically such defendants would be held for the duration of the trial. The defendant would remain in unconvicted detention until all appeals were completed, in a jail or house of detention rather than a regular prison.

The status of unconvicted detention provides a number of legal rights that a prisoner serving a sentence does not enjoy. Prisoners in unconvicted detention are permitted one visitor a day from virtually any-one (unless they are being held incommunicado), while prisoners serving sentences can have only one visit a month from designated immediate family members. Persons in unconvicted detention also enjoy extensive mail privileges, wear regular clothing, and may receive certain items from the outside. While they are generally held in solitary confinement under quite harsh and rigid conditions, as opposed to the communal life of the regular prison, these communications privileges make unconvicted detention far preferable to serving regular prison time for both the defendant and the family. Moreover, the judge has discretion to count much of the time spent in unconvicted detention as time served when setting the length of the sentence. For persons facing a lengthy prison sentence, and particularly for those facing the death penalty, the goal of the Kyūen strategy is to keep the person in unconvicted detention for as long as possible.

Even in a sensational case with the potential for a long sentence or the death penalty, most Japanese private criminal lawyers would not pursue such a course because it is time-consuming and costly, and does not lead to a shorter sentence. They would still advise the defendant facing such charges to plead guilty and seek the court's mercy through contrition. In fact, the full trial strategy is only really possible for the types of political defendants the Kyūen system serves. The ordinary criminal route depends upon the defendant pleading guilty and seeking the court's mercy, but the Kyūen defendants do not want to plead guilty because they believe their actions were committed for political or ideological reasons that justify special legal treatment. The defendants want a full trial in order to present their political rationale, even if the court is unlikely to be persuaded by it.

Moreover, the Kyūen strategy of extending the trial and appeals as long as possible is really only possible in cases where there is a dedicated support group to help the defendant survive years of unconvicted detention in solitary confinement. It is unlikely that even the most loving and supportive family could provide the amount of regular visits, written communication, and external support that a person in long-term unconvicted detention needs, but this becomes manageable with a support group sharing the burden. The contrast is most stark for those anticipating the death penalty, since persons awaiting the death penalty are also kept in solitary confinement in the same facilities as persons in unconvicted detention, but without their communications privileges. Those whose death penalty sentence has been confirmed but who are awaiting execution must spend their time in solitary confinement with only one visit from close family per month, and one seven page letter out permitted per month. Some New Left defendants have been waiting on Death Row for two decades. In several cases, support group members have participated in marriages or legal adult adoptions in order to ensure that a prisoner with a lengthy sentence or someone awaiting the death penalty will have sufficient outside support from someone who is legally permitted to visit and correspond with the prisoner. Visitation privileges were somewhat relaxed for persons awaiting the death penalty in 2007 to permit weekly visits from a slightly wider range of visitors, but the prisoners' isolation remains severe.

The trial strategy that will provide the most desirable conditions of greater outside contact for the defendant and greater personal contact for the parent is to use Kyūen lawyers and mount a full political trial with the aid of a support group. The parents may hire private lawyers who are willing to work with a Kyūen lawyer to provide the necessary specialized expertise for the case, and they may also be paying regular fees to the Kyūen lawyer, as opposed to having counsel appointed by the court. In any case, they need to have lawyers who understand and can implement the strategy, and who will work with a support group to facilitate it. The support group also provides some paralegal expertise and services, which helps to reduce the costs of the extended legal proceedings.

Yet above and beyond the attractiveness of the Kyūen legal strategy for Sensational Trial Crises, the family members also are pulled toward working with Kyūen because of their own needs. Family members who are suddenly caught up in a Sensational Crime Crisis face tremendous pressure from the mass media when the story breaks, especially if the crime has been causing a sensation well before any perpetrators are arrested. Far more devastating than even the mass media hysteria is the hostility the family receives from the people around them, as well as from the police. By following family members constantly, conducting noisy and highly visible searches of family residences and workplaces, and investigating friends, neighbors, and casual acquaintances of the entire family, the police contribute to public marking of the family's pariah status, which is reinforced by inaccurate reports in the media that may also come from police sources.

The resulting hysteria generates open hostility toward the family, including hate mail and hate graffiti. That sort of public rejection and hostility is painful to bear in any society, but ordinary middle-class people in Japanese society may feel particularly vulnerable and defenseless in the face of such social rejection. In late May 1972, three young Japanese men who had secretly gone to the Middle East a few months earlier, caused shockwaves around the world when they attacked the baggage claim area of the Tel Aviv (Lod) Airport in Israel, killing twenty-six people and wounding seventy-five. Although two of the Japanese were killed in the attack and the third was captured and put on trial in Israel, the Japanese media were soon full of stories about the search for an accomplice who had returned to Japan before the attack, Himori Kōyū.

While police searched for him, his family in Akita was besieged by police and reporters. The hysteria continued after his arrest a few weeks later. His mother reports,

> The incident that really pushed me into thinking [that I was born under a bad star] was the Tel Aviv Incident in May 1972. The police came every day, saying that Kōyū was involved in it, and they pestered [her married son and his family] as well. Because of Kōyū they had to go to the police station and the the lawyer's office every day, and I had to do a lot of it myself. (Himori 2005)

Although Himori had not participated in the attack, he had been involved in the preparations, and he was deeply troubled that the plan had gone awry and a large number of Puerto Rican Christians, making a pilgrimage to Israel, had been killed. The charge against him was simply a passport violation because he had failed to report his previous conviction on his passport application. Himori confessed, and has given his own reasons for doing so. It is not clear whether family pressures played a role in his decision, but he received only a short jail sentence (Himori 1999). However, as soon as he was released from jail, he went underground and did not surface or contact his family for the next fourteen years. Even after he returned to normal life, this son's behavior and the fear that he might do something terrible again consumed his mother's life.

> For me now, my greatest wish is that Kōyū would settle down before I die. This is a problem I cannot forget for a single day, rain or shine. Since this happened with Kōyū I cannot go out where other people are gathered. I cannot overcome my fate and resolve this, and nobody else can possibly understand my sadness and anguish.
>
> Today I pray to Buddha that he won't cause trouble for the other children, and every day all I can think of is how I can bear it. I ask only that Kōyū not cause any extreme incident. (Himori 2005, p. 23)

In the hostile environment surrounding a Sensational Crime, Kyūen support groups, and parents groups in particular, may be the only people who offer kindness and support to the beleaguered and bewildered family members. That support, in turn, helps them extend support to their children who have been arrested and are charged with a sensational crime. This process is illustrated most clearly in the case of the Higashi Ajia Hannichi Busō Sensen [East Asia Anti-Japanese Armed Front] bombing group.

For a six month period in 1974–75, Japan was rocked by a series of time bomb attacks on corporate and industrial targets for which a shadowy group called "Higashi Ajia Hannichi Busō Sensen" (nicknamed

Hannichi) took responsibility through notices sent out after each bombing. The first and most devastating attack involved two bombs planted at the Mitsubishi Heavy Industries headquarters building in downtown Tokyo, in which eight people were killed and scores more injured. The remaining bombings in the series were carried out at night in presumably empty buildings, but one other attack injured a night watchman. The bombings appeared random to the nervous public, although the group chose its targets after careful historical research and the attacks were intended as retribution for the companies' exploitation of Asian workers during the war and their continuing exploitive practices in Asian countries.

In direct and deliberate contrast to the Red Army, which began as a public insurgency group and only gradually went underground, Hannichi was deeply underground from its inception. It was composed of very small cells that operated semi-independently. The members were former students who had strong political concerns but had not been prominent participants in student groups. They had regular employment, maintained regular contact with their families, and did not dress or talk like stereotypical radical students. They were invisible in a society where police thought they knew all the markers for New Left students who were likely to commit violent acts. As the bombings continued without any break in the case, the public and mass media demanded ever more shrilly that the police catch the criminals. Finally, eight suspected members of the group were arrested in simultaneous early morning raids in May 1975. Another was named and put on the nationwide wanted list but was not caught until seven years later. After his recent release from prison, he wrote in the support group newsletter,

> Every member of Higashi Ajia Hannichi Busō Sensen had a family. Naturally the members were shunned as traitors and persecuted, but our families were also shunned and persecuted in the same way. In my own family, although my father was the first son, he was not even invited to his own father's funeral. How painful that must have been. They were also harassed by the neighbors countless times. One morning after a snowfall, the snow was mounded up in front of our house and a pile of dog dung was left in it with the word "hikokumin" (traitor).
>
> In the midst of that storm, the Hannichi families persevered without being crushed. I didn't know about the storm the Hannichi families were experiencing. But now [that I'm out of prison], I hear about it from my mother every day (Ukagami Juichi, "Shako no rihabiri nikki (sono jūichi)." *Shienren nyūsu* no. 260, May 29, 2004, pp. 5–6)

Although the members of Hannichi were aware of Kyūen Renraku Sentā, some of the cells were particularly nihilistic, believing that if they were arrested it would be the end of revolutionary activity in Japan. They did not look forward to continuing their resistance in the criminal justice system, but instead carried cyanide capsules so they could commit suicide if they were arrested. One of the eight Hannichi members arrested, Saitō Nodoka, was able to swallow his cyanide capsule and died in police custody within a few hours after his arrest. The others were prevented from using their capsules. Without a strong commitment to the Kyūen mantra of refusing to talk, some soon succumbed to interrogation pressures and gave incriminating statements.

However, Kyūen Renraku Sentā and other support organizations were involved in the case from the day of the arrests. Kyūen lawyers were experienced in dealing with the very severe charges possible under Japan's explosives control law, which dates from anarchist bombings in the Meiji era and can carry the death penalty. Kyūen staff were also well aware of the tremendous public pressure to find the bombers in this case, and already had experience with suicides of both prisoners and family members in sensational cases. As soon as they learned of the Saitō suicide from news reports on the morning of the arrests, they formed a forensic investigation team and demanded to conduct an investigation of the circumstances of the death (Kyūen Sentā, #74, 6/10/1975:1; reprinted in Kyūen Shukusatsuban Kankō Iinkai 1977). In addition to providing lawyers for some of the arrestees, they were able to establish contact with the families by the day after the arrests and quickly formed a parents' group.

A week later tragedy struck. Kyūen Renraku Sentā received a phone call from the police in a regional city where one of the families lived, reporting that a woman had been killed in a train accident. She had jumped in front of a train during rush hour, a common method of suicide in Japan, and the Kyūen hotline phone number 591–1301 was written on her left arm. The woman was Arai Nahoko, the elder sister of one of the arrestees, Arai Mariko. Two Kyūen staff members and a lawyer went immediately to help the family. They went with family members the next morning to identify the body, and saw for themselves the Kyūen phone number written on the woman's arm. Vowing that his daughter's death would not be in vain, the angry father came to Tokyo and participated the following day in a press conference at which the newly formed family group and the lawyers chastised the media and police for their harassment of family members and the hysterical coverage that had led to a family member's suicide (Kyūen Sentā, #74, 6/10/75:1; reprinted in Kyūen Shukusatsuban Kankō Iinkai 1977).

Complicating matters further for the Arai family, there was very little evidence to connect the daughter who had been arrested, Mariko, to the bombings. She had been living with her parents in a provincial city when the bombings were carried out in Tokyo, but she had known other members of the group and had done some research for them on pharmaceutical compounds. Despite the lack of evidence linking her to the bombings, she was charged under the explosives control law with having provided "spiritual support" to the group. She and the two other women in the Hannichi group proved to be adept at resistance within the criminal justice system during their trial, carrying out hunger strikes and deliberately violating other restrictions in the women's quarters of Tokyo House of Detention. Arai Mariko received an eight year sentence for her "spiritual support" of the bombing group, but ended up serving twelve years in all because of her resistance and the long appeal process (Arai 1986).

Athough neither of their daughters was centrally involved in the Hannichi bombings, the Arai parents became stalwart figures in the Hannichi parents group. This parents group has remained active for nearly thirty years, supporting one another and participating in activities with the broader Hannichi support organization. For the decade from 1995 to 2005, the group was reinvigorated by the trial of Ekita Yukiko, a Hannichi member who was arrested with the rest of the group in 1975, but was released "extrajudicially" in an international hostage-taking incident staged in 1977 by the Japanese Red Army. She went with them to the Middle East and subsequently became a member of the Japanese Red Army. In 1995, she was discovered in Romania and deported to Japan, where her trial resumed where it had left off, after a lapse of twenty years. The renewed trial activity, coupled with Ekita's lively personality, reinvigorated a support group that had primarily been involved in anti-death penalty campaigns and various side issues after the main Hannichi trials had ended.

I was present at the final session of Ekita's first trial in 2002, when the court's decision was announced. Support group members had come from all over Japan to attend the trial session and a meeting of the support group afterwards. Three elderly people sat together in the support group meeting, laughing and joking with each other. They were Mr. and Mrs. Arai and Ekita Yukiko's mother. Later in the afternoon, I ran into the Arai family again in the visitors' waiting room at Tokyo House of Detention, where they were waiting to visit Ekita (field notes, Ekita trial, support group meeting, and prison waiting room 7/4/02). Despite the shock and tragedy that the Hannichi Sensational Crime Crisis had brought to their own family, they had found strength and solace in the

Hannichi support group and had gone on to provide support and care to others.

By contrast, families that did not participate in the Kyūen support network are sometimes unable to reconcile with the child who has committed a Sensational Crime. One person who was involved in several international incidents connected to the Japanese Red Army remained in exile until 2000, when he was deported to Japan for arrest and trial. Although he spoke fondly of his father at his first court appearance and writes regularly to his family in northern Japan, the family refuses to have any contact with him. His support group sends newsletters to them regularly, and intermediaries have tried to make contact, but his father is adamant. The issue is not so much the son's acts themselves, as the damage the resulting publicity and police pressure cause to the family. The ramifications even led to a brother's divorce. His father's position is that while the son's acts might be forgiven, the harm the son's actions caused to the rest of the family is simply unforgivable (field notes from joint prison visit 6/24/05).

In summary, the Sensational Crime Crisis placed tremendous pressure on families because of the serious charges their child faced, the relentless hounding by the police and mass media, and the hostility of people around them. In these circumstances, the Kyūen trial strategy appeared to be the most effective way to maintain contact with their child for a longer period of time, an advantage that increased with the severity of the potential sentence to be served. Perhaps even more important, the Kyūen volunteer support system provided a safe haven for the families where they were treated with warmth and dignity by people who understood their plight. When they were rejected by former friends and associates, and blamed for what their children had done, they were able to channel their pain and energy into volunteer support activities. By supporting other prisoners in addition to their own children, they could feel that they were contributing to society despite its rejection of them.

Cooperating to Reclaim Stranded Children

The Stranded Child Crisis arose in the mid-1990s as a consequence of the formation of new families of procreation by activists in exile. Their children were born overseas to Japanese parents and thus had a strong claim to Japanese citizenship, which is based on descent and manifested by registration in the family registry of an existing Japanese family. Because of the parents' status as wanted persons, their foreign-born children were not registered at birth, and they also usually had no claim to citizenship in their country of birth or residence. Legally, they were stateless persons.

Prior to the early 1990s, families and supporters in Japan did not know about most of these children until the arrest of an activist parent led to a Stranded Child Crisis. In some later cases, the children were already adults, but they were still stranded by their statelessness and could not travel to Japan to claim their citizenship without assistance. Resolution of these crises required an unusual multifaceted cooperation between social actors who had been opposing each other for decades. Activists, their families, the state, and the support organizations all cooperated to bring these stateless children to Japan.

The initial groundwork for returning stranded children began in the early 1990s when the exiled Red Army Faction hijackers in North Korea revealed that they had both Japanese wives and stateless children living with them in North Korea. Most of the wives had left Japan on valid passports many years earlier and had traveled secretly to North Korea. Japanese authorities had recalled their passports in the mid-1980s when they suspected that the women were in North Korea, but had not connected the women to the Yodogo group of the Red Army Faction until Kim Il Jong himself revealed the connection inadvertently in a meeting with Japanese newspaper reporters. As part of an overall effort to help these exiles and their families return to Japan, the director of Kyūen Renraku Sentā began discussing the problem with officials in the Foreign Ministry to determine the necessary procedures. Progress for this group was complicated by the absence of diplomatic relations between Japan and North Korea, and the special demands of the hijackers concerning the conditions and desired sequence of the returns. It was also not clear what obstacles the North Korean government might put up to prevent the return of the hijackers and their families.

While the North Korean problem was still at the research and negotiation stage, a true Stranded Child Crisis arose in a completely different quarter, when a woman named Yoshimura Kazue was suddenly arrested in Peru and deported to Japan in 1996. Yoshimura had been on Interpol wanted lists since the mid-1970s because the Japanese government suspected that she had played an intermediary role in an international hostage-taking incident carried out by Japanese activists in the Hague in 1974. A European language student, Yoshimura went abroad initially on a legal Japanese passport and visa, but had ties to the Japanese group that became the Japanese Red Army. After the Japanese government made her a wanted person and rendered her passport unusable, she ended up staying with the Japanese Red Army in the Middle East. Twenty years later, Japanese authorities discovered her living in Lima, Peru. Through cooperation with local Peruvian authorities she was arrested on the street in Lima and immediately deported to Japan, where she was arrested and charged with passport violations.

Kyūen Renraku Sentā and the support group Kikokusha no Saiban o Kangaeru Kai, which had been formed several years earlier to handle the influx of arrested returnees from the Japanese Red Army group based in the Middle East, immediately swung into action to assist Yoshimura. The Kyūen lawyer who was sent to interview her discovered that she was in a state of panic because she had left a fourteen year old boy stranded in Peru. The boy was not her own child, but was the son of Ekita Yukiko and another Japanese Red Army member. When the boy was about five, he had been entrusted to Yoshimura's care so his parents could continue their political activities. Yoshimura took the boy to Peru so he could grow up in a safe environment, in a place where a Japanese child could blend into the local Japanese population. In addition to worrying about his immediate safety and care in Peru, Yoshimura was deeply distressed because she had failed in her responsibility to protect him.

Ekita had been arrested and deported to Japan two years earlier, and was in Tokyo House of Detention and on trial herself. To complicate matters further, the boy was living in Peru under an assumed name with false documents. He knew he was the son of Japanese Red Army members, but had been carefully trained not to reveal his real identity to anyone or to cooperate with any strangers. Once it was clear that the boy was safely in the custody of Peruvian child welfare authorities, the support groups settled down to the task of getting him to Japan. He could not leave Peru and enter Japan until he had legal travel documents in his real name, issued by the Japanese government. Japanese Foreign Ministry officials could not issue these documents until the boy had been registered in a family register in Japan. And in order for that to happen, the relationship between the boy and his Japanese parent had to be established to the satisfaction of the Japanese authorities, since he had not been registered at a Japanese consulate or embassy at the time of his birth.

Ekita immediately acknowledged that the boy was her son, but refused to name his father. Hence, the boy would need to be entered in her own family's register, but she first needed to prove that he was her child. Following Japanese custom, she had saved his umbilical cord and reported that it could be found in the belongings she had in her possession when she was arrested. She also offered to participate in a DNA test that would establish her relationship to the boy, but prison officials refused to permit a DNA test. Instead, Ekita was interviewed by Japanese child welfare officials and wrote a deposition stating that she was the boy's birth mother. In the deposition, she explained that they had left Beirut during the civil war when he was a baby, and his birth record had been destroyed in the war.

The Kyūen lawyers and staff began processing the necessary official paperwork to get the boy registered in the family register and then obtain temporary travel documents for him. Ekita's parents, long connected to the Hannichi parents support group, were happy to enter their grandchild into the family register, but they were elderly farmers and could not take care of the boy after he was brought to Japan. The child knew spoken Japanese, but could not read or write very well, and had been educated in Spanish. Both his mother and his primary caregiver were in jail, and no other family members were available to take him in.

Since it was Ekita's child, it became a problem for the special joint support group that had been set up for Ekita's trial, which was composed of members from both the Hannichi support organization and the Kikokusha no Saiban o Kangaeru Kai support group that handled Red Army returnees. The group wrestled with it at a meeting, and subsequently the support group's leader, who had a teenaged son of his own, agreed to take the boy into his home (field notes, Yuki Q meeting, June 21, 1996). The next issue was how to get the boy from Peru to Japan, which was both a logistic and a financial problem. The money materialized, and the experienced woman lawyer who was handling Yoshimura's case arranged to go to Peru and bring the boy back. To do so, she had to learn from Yoshimura the secret code that would let the boy know that it was okay to go with her. She also took along letters from his two "mothers" to establish her authenticity.

The boy stayed in the support group leader's family for the next several years, and had the usual school difficulties of a Japanese returnee child. He was permitted to visit his mother regularly at Tokyo House of Detention, and shyly celebrated his sixteenth birthday with the support group. When Yoshimura was released after completing her sentence for passport violations, she moved in with the support group leader's family and the boy until she had a job and could afford to support herself and the boy in a separate apartment.

A few years later in November 2000, exiled Japanese Red Army leader Shigenobu Fusako was arrested in Osaka and brought to Tokyo for trial on charges related to planning of the Hague Incident and the usual passport violations. Although she followed the Kyūen strategy and used a Kyūen lawyer for her trial, a separate trial support organization was formed for her that was not connected to the Kikokusha group. While still being held incommunicado at Tokyo police headquarters, she managed to publish a book with the help of her lawyer. It was based in part on depositions she wrote to establish Japanese citizenship for her daughter Mei, who was by then a young woman in her twenties (Shigenobu 2001).

The lawyer, the same woman who had brought Ekita's son home from Peru, then traveled to Lebanon and handled the processing to bring both Shigenobu's daughter Mei and Yoshimura's own daughter Midori back to Japan. This time the key piece of evidence linking mother and daughter was not the umbilical cord, but a photo showing only the back of Shigenobu and her daughter's heads, but not their faces (for security reasons), which mother and daughter both carried for many years. Mei and Midori, who was three years younger, had been raised together like sisters from childhood, and educated in French and English schools. They had also lived with Ekita's son as their "younger brother" when he was small, with other Red Army exiles as their extended family (Shigenobu 2002). The two "sisters" became regular observers at Shigenobu's trial (field notes, Shigenobu trial sessions, Tokyo District Court 6/26/2001, 6/28/2001, 6/28,2002, 6/23/2003). Shigenobu's first trial ended in December 2005, but she remained in court-ordered incommunicado status until June 2007, when testimony in the appeal trial ended. Since Shigenobu's parents are both deceased, her adult daughter and sister were the only persons allowed to visit her, aside from her lawyers, for over six years (Steinhoff 2009 forthcoming).

Although the Stranded Child Crisis for these three Japanese Red Army children and their families proceeded smoothly and cooperatively, one set of children stranded in North Korea became embroiled in a very difficult family conflict that greatly complicated their retrieval. At the time Shibata Yasuhiro was arrested and put on trial in Japan in the late 1980s, no one knew that the exiles in North Korea had Japanese families with them. In his court testimony and at support group meetings, Shibata's father frequently expressed his wish that his son would complete his sentence, get married, and have a family so he could live like a normal person of his age. After Shibata was arrested, the police investigation led to a woman running a bar in Yokosuka to whom he had made some phone calls. The mass media intimated that she was a North Korean spy, but she denied it vociferously and even sued the *Asahi Shinbun* for slander (Yao 2002).

Two years later, however, when the existence of the group's wives became public, it turned out that this woman, Yao Megumi, was in fact Shibata's wife. Both had been sent on semi-independent missions in Japan, leaving behind their two young daughters in the care of the group, which lived comfortably in the suburbs outside of Pyongyang in a private compound staffed with North Korean cooks, nursemaids, and drivers. The adult members of this exile group were frequently sent out of the country on special missions, while the children stayed behind, apparently to ensure that the parents would return (Takazawa 1998).

However, once Shibata had been arrested and identified, he could not return to North Korea, and neither could Yao, since she was also being watched by the Japanese police.

Although they had been conducted with considerable ceremony in North Korea, none of the hijackers' marriages were legal in Japan because they had not been properly registered. Yao felt she had been forced into an unhappy marriage to Shibata by the North Korean agents who lured her to Pyongyang, so once he had been arrested in Japan, she was happy to leave him. At the same time, she was very anxious to get her stranded children out of North Korea. For several years, she cooperated with the Kyūen Renraku Sentā administrator who was working with the group in North Korea on arrangements to bring them all to Japan, but the publicly announced plans to bring the children to Japan kept falling through. Despite the fact that both parents of the Shibata children were in Japan, the group in North Korea wanted some of their own older children to return to Japan first. Frustrated with the lack of progress, Yao tried making her own arrangements. She had the two girls entered in her family register, but the group in North Korea objected strongly to that arrangement as socially disgraceful for the children because of its implication of illegitimacy. They wanted the girls to be entered in Shibata's family register and returned to him.

In desperation, Yao filed suit in Tokyo District Court against the leader of the group in North Korea, demanding that he return her children. To coincide with the civil trial, Yao also published a sensational series of articles in a Japanese weekly claiming that she was lured to North Korea under false pretense and forced to marry Shibata, who had been a bad husband who beat her (Yao 1998a; Yao 1998b; Yao 1998c). The first trial session was a circus. Although Yao herself did not attend, the civil trial opening session was followed by several press conferences by the various parties. Her two daughters had sent an angry public letter in which they claimed their mother had abandoned them by not returning to North Korea, and said they no longer considered her their mother. They criticized her sharply for showing disrespect toward "the mothers who raised us," meaning the other women in the hijackers' group in North Korea. By then out of prison and living with family members in Kansai, Shibata came up to Tokyo for the civil trial session in support of the North Korean group. He was primarily concerned that his daughters' forceful public rejection of their mother, which he regarded as irrevocable, would later cause them psychological damage (field notes: trial, press conferences, nijikai, and phone call from Shibata, 11/18,1998).

The strange trial soon collapsed amid rumors that Yao's lawyer had been threatened by thugs for the other side. Five years later, the two adult daughters were finally brought to Japan after they had been reregistered in their father's family register and received new travel documents, and after several other children had been brought from North Korea.

In both exile groups the children were raised in a communal living situation that permitted some parents to remain politically active internationally while others helped raise their children. The Stranded Child Crises involved three generations of family members plus some of these surrogate family members who had shared in the children's upbringing. In the one Stranded Child case that involved a family conflict, the source of the problem was the involvement of the other members of the exile group in North Korea, which wanted to control the terms of the children's return.

Perhaps most remarkable in these crises is the behavior of the state. State authorities in the same Foreign Ministry that seeks to track down the exiled parents anywhere in the world and bring them home so they can be prosecuted also willingly cooperate to process the papers necessary to bring their stateless children home to Japan. To do so, they have to interact with representatives of Kyūen Renraku Sentā and Kyūen lawyers. Although at one level these people have been on opposite sides of a social conflict for decades, at another level they are all Japanese of relatively similar background and education, who act according to the law to resolve specific problems.

Discussion and Conclusions

We have now examined both the general circumstances and some specific examples of the three types of arrest crises. There was a relatively low probability of preexisting family conflict arising from students' participation in protest activity prior to the Mass Arrest Crisis. That crisis created considerable potential for family conflict over whether the parent should cooperate with the child's choice to fight the arrest, or cooperate with the police to pressure the child to leave the movement. Families that successfully pressured the child to leave the movement risked continuing resentment from the child, who experienced feelings of guilt, failure, and alienation from friends. Those who remained in the movement experienced less family conflict overall, because parents and child had cooperated in their handling of the crisis.

Sensational Crimes Crises placed tremendous strain on families and resulted in some family tragedies, but the circumstances also encouraged parents to meet their own needs by supporting the child's resistance strategy, thereby reducing family conflict and increasing family support for the child. The Stranded Child Crisis involved a different dynamic, in which the state and support organizations cooperated to resolve the situation, but family conflicts arose if other parties that had control of the stranded children did not cooperate.

While the three Japanese types of family arrest crisis are in some respects specific to the Japanese legal system, similar patterns can be found in the other contemporaneous New Left protest cycles in Western countries. Studies of American student activists of the 1960s protest era have found that the more dedicated activists tended to come from liberal families that either supported or did not strongly oppose their children's political activism (Flacks and Whalen 1989). In an unusually well-designed study, D. McAdam and R. Paulson (1993) found that among young people who had been accepted for the high risk Freedom Summer project to register Blacks to vote in Mississippi, those who actually ended up participating in Freedom Summer had not only other friends who went, but parental support. Although the circumstances are different, the nature of family relations seems similar to those found in the Mass Arrest and Sensational Crimes Crises in Japan.

While there was much less use of exile to escape repression in the United States, the underground movement was quite parallel to that in Japan and involved children raised in semi-communal settings. In a kind of fusion of the Sensational Crimes and Stranded Child Crises, there are numerous instances in the United States in which children of activists serving lengthy prison sentences for Sensational Crimes have been quietly raised by other activist families, often with strong support from their grandparents (Zwerman 1994).

These cases of family crisis among New Left activists also reinforce certain enduring aspects of our understanding of Japanese family relations and interpersonal dynamics. It is absolutely clear that the Japanese police in 1968–1975 used the same tactics as they had in 1928–1935 to induce committed young political activists to give up their resistance to the state (Steinhoff 1991). Their most powerful weapon was the emotional ties binding the family, whose strings they plucked like accomplished koto players. They tried to break the young activists' resistance with images of the shame and pain they were causing their parents, and they tried to enlist the aid of crying mothers to beg their children to do what the police asked.

Young people in the late 1960s were perhaps almost as emotionally vulnerable to these themes as they had been forty years earlier. What had changed was the postwar Constitution and educational reforms, upon which the New Left's volunteer support system built its key weapon of resistance, the refusal to talk to the police. That new culture of constitutional rights and resistance in turn gave parents a way to channel their desire to help their child into support for the resistance strategy. A powerful side benefit of doing so was the emotional support the parents found within the New Left's volunteer support community, which welcomed them and offered them sympathy and understanding when the mass media, the police, and the public rejected them as bad parents who were responsible for their children's actions. Without the New Left's support system it is not just the activist children who would have capitulated. As the instances of suicide demonstrate, without the support system even more family members undoubtedly would have buckled under the tremendous social pressure.

Even the handling of the Stranded Child Crises reflects the Japanese state's fundamental understanding of the relationship between families and the state. Neighbors might call the families of the Hannichi bombers *hikokumin* or traitors, but the state recognized the citizenship claim of their stateless children, as long as they could be linked to an existing Japanese family lineage through registration in a family register. Once that was established, the children were *kokumin*, entitled to the full protection of Japanese law.

While the foreign ministry's cooperation in the Stranded Child Crises demonstrates that the Japanese state is not monolithic, it should be emphasized that the state continues to pursue the remaining exiled members of Japanese radical groups from the 1960s and 1970s, as part of their cooperation in international antiterrorism agreements. Once found, the exiles are prosecuted vigorously in Japan using the most serious charges possible, even when the alleged crimes were committed entirely on foreign soil. Indeed, the Japanese criminal justice system's handling of these special "political" cases has become more severe in some respects, with some chilling parallels to American handling of suspected terrorists post 9/11. All of the procedures I have described for the 1960s and 1970s still prevail, and the practice of holding incommunicado persons who refuse to cooperate with the police and prosecutors has been broadened and extended.

Chapter 6

Is "Japan" Still A Big Family?

Nationality and Citizenship at the
Edge of the Japanese Archipelago

Mariko Asano Tamanoi

Introduction

September 26, 2004. "Seven more hits in eight more games, and Ichirō of
the Seattle Mariners will be the record holder!" so exclaims the anchor-
man for the NHK news broadcast. And so it is in Japan these days that
the news has been completely dominated by Ichirō. How many times
did Ichirō score a hit? How many more times will he score a hit today?
The Japanese audience seems thrilled by his extraordinary athleticism.
Even more so, the Japanese media speaks of Ichirō as if he were "Japan's
last samurai": he hardly talks, hardly smiles, but demonstrates his ability
through actions. Ichirō is a Japanese national and Japanese citizen, but
plays overseas in the United States. What explains his unprecedented
popularity *in Japan*? Is it because of his obvious giftedness as a major
sports figure, which bespeaks of a sense of national pride transmitted
internationally? Is this because of his stark shining contrast to the current state of chaos within Japanese baseball? Is this because he carries
the best essence of "being Japanese" whatever that may be? When will
Ichirō's popularity wane? When he can no longer play as good or better
as he does now? When will he become more "Americanized?" When
he decides not to return to Japan? Or perhaps it may happen when
he renounces his Japanese citizenship and chooses to become a U.S.
citizen instead?

In this chapter, I will examine one particular kind of conflict situations, in which the Japanese individuals, who stand on the edge of the

111

Japanese archipelagos, violate the still dominant perception among the Japanese populace about Japan, that is, "Japan is a big family." These Japanese individuals need not be as talented as Ichirō. Rather, any Japanese individual can potentially cause this conflict situation. I am aware, however, that such a category as "Japanese nationals" or "Japanese citizens" is artificial that emerged along with the formation of Japan as a modern nation-state. While "Japan" in this chapter refers to the current sovereign territory of Japan, the perception among the Japanese populace about Japan has never been unified or static. After all, the notion that "Japan is a big family" is a historical and rather recent construct, and this notion in itself has been changing. Therefore, by asking "is Japan *still* a big family?", I aim to take a historical approach to this particular kind of conflict situations.

Unfortunately (for the fans of Ichirō), this chapter is not about Ichirō. At this moment, relationships between the Japanese public and Ichirō do not present conflict situations at all. The television audience rejoice at his athletic prowess because he is unmistakably "Japanese" or the son of a family called "Japan" (that he does not speak English well, or that his dog has a Japanese name, Ikkyū, seem to please the Japanese audience). Still, as a member of the American baseball team, he stands at the edge of Japan: there is no guarantee that he will ever return to Japanese baseball. We may therefore anticipate that conflict situations may develop in the future between the Japanese populace and Ichirō. This chapter, however, examines the conflict situations that already occurred and have still been developing since the end of World War II, between the children of the Japanese parents who emigrated to Northeast China (Manchuria) as agrarian colonists in the age of empire (from the late nineteenth century to 1945) and the Japanese people who had remained in Japan proper during the same period of time. Before introducing the protagonists of this chapter, however, a brief history of Manchuria is in order.

Manchuria today is unquestionably part of the sovereign territory of the People's Republic of China, and one of the thriving centers of industrialization. As it is located in the northeastern region of China, the Chinese government calls the area *Dongbei*, Northeast China. The region, however, was under Japan's influence throughout the age of empire. Japan's victory over China in 1895 and yet another victory over Russia in 1905, enabled Japan to gain control of the southern tip of the Liaodong peninsula in southern Manchuria. In 1931, Japan further invaded into Manchuria and established Manchukuo, a de facto colony of Japan, and presented it to the international community as a modern independent nation-state. Finally, in 1937, Japan started a war against

China proper (south of the Great Wall), which eventually led Japan to the war against the Allied forces from 1941 to 1945.

With Japan's capitulation in World War II, Manchukuo, which had lasted only for thirteen years, perished overnight together with the rest of the Japanese Empire. In the aftermath of Japan's defeat, about 2.2 million Japanese, both soldiers and civilians, were stranded in Manchuria (Kōsei-shō 1997, 11, 32). Among them, there were about three hundred twenty-two thousand agrarian colonists (Young 1998, 328). The repatriation of these Japanese farmers, who lost the state's protection, was extremely arduous for the following reasons. First, they were destined to suffer once the empire collapsed. That is to say, when sending farmers to Manchuria, Japanese military placed them near the border with the Soviet Union for strategic reasons. Without knowing military's intentions, agrarian colonists planned to settle in Manchuria to help create the Japanese Empire. After the onset of the war with the United States, however, the Japanese army began a systematic draft of the male agrarian colonists. This mobilization eventually became "bottom-scraping (*nekosogi*)," and radically altered the human geography in northern Manchuria. Those who were left behind were largely women, children, and the elderly. Instead of protecting these civilians, Japanese army utilized them to create a buffer zone against the Soviet Union's imminent attack. As the army correctly predicted, the Soviet Union invaded Manchuria on August 9, 1945. The Japanese men who had remained in northern Manchuria were taken by the Soviets to labor camps in Siberia. The local peasants, who were once themselves displaced by the Japanese settlers, turned their rage against Japanese colonists. The civil war between the Communist and Nationalist forces in China, both of which tried to mobilize Japanese civilians for their military operations, created more confusion among the Japanese stranded in Manchuria. Severe winters and poor hygienic conditions caused malnutrition, epidemics, and other diseases. Among those who were not mobilized, namely, women, children, and the elderly, about 60 percent died before reaching Japan's shores. The rest took months, years, and decades to return home. The survival rate among the farmers who were mobilized was, ironically, higher: although many of them were taken to Siberia as prisoners of war by the Soviets, more than 70 percent returned safely to Japan, for they were better protected by international treaties.

Here, what captures my attention are the children of Japanese mothers, themselves wives of agrarian colonists, who, in their own words, "entrusted," "gave up," "sold," or "abandoned" their loved ones to Chinese couples—the strategy these mothers took to save not only their children, but also themselves. If these mothers survived, they returned to Japan without children. The children who had remained in China, then, were raised by Chinese adoptive parents, attended schools in China, married Chinese citizens, and have raised their own families in China. Largely due to the state of diplomatic relationship between Japan and China, these children were not allowed to return to Japan until the mid-1970s. It is believed that approximately thirty thousand Japanese nationals, called in Japanese *zanryū koji* ("the orphans who have remained behind"), were still in China in 1972 when Japan normalized relations with the People's Republic of China (Yampol 2005, 129).[1]

In this chapter, three groups of people appear. First are former agrarian colonists who were repatriated from Manchuria soon after Japan's capitulation, between 1946 and 1949, and who have lived in Japan since then. Although they were called *hikiage-sha* ("those who were repatriated from overseas") for quite some time after their return to Japan, now that more than half a century has passed since the war's end, many of them identify themselves as such only in their memories. Second are the protagonists of this chapter, *zanryū koji* (whom I shall call "orphans" in the rest of this chapter), or the children of Japanese colonists who had been left in China but who began returning to Japan in the mid-1970s. Third is not an actual group of people: it is an abstract entity called Japan or the Japanese mainstream society. Conflict situations occurred and have been occurring: (1) between *hikiage-sha* and the Japanese mainstream society (conflict situations 1); (2) between *hikiage-sha* and orphans (conflict situations 2); and (3) between orphans and the Japanese mainstream society (conflict situations 3). To deal with these complex conflict situations, I will structure this paper in the following. First, I will examine conflict situations 1 that have developed historically since 1945. Second, through ethnography, I will examine conflict situations 3. Here, I understand *hikiage-sha* as middlemen who could potentially mediate the conflicts between orphans and the Japanese mainstream society. Thus, examining conflict situations 3, I must inevitably deal with conflict situations 2. Writing ethnography about orphans turned out to be particularly difficult, largely because most of them do not speak the language of their parents—Japanese. For the recent returnees from China, who are already in their sixties and seventies, learning a new language is by no means easy. Hence, Japanese people hardly listen to the genuine voices of orphans. Instead, they tend to listen to the voices constructed by Japan's media, which is notorious for creating the image of Japan as a big family. It is under these circumstances in which I stepped into some families of orphans to explore their complicated positions in contemporary Japan. Thus, this chapter deals with two kinds of families, the family of an orphan that consists of both Japanese and Chinese nationals, and the family of the nation-state of Japan.

Conflict Situations 1

First, let me go back to the seventeenth century. One of the orders issued by the Tokugawa Shogunate in the early seventeenth century has the following provision.

> Japanese subjects who have resided abroad shall be put to death if they return to Japan. Exception is made for those who have resided abroad for less than five years and have been unavoidably detained. They shall be exempt from punishment, but if they attempt to go abroad again they are to be put to death. (Sansom 1963, 36)

At the onset of the isolation period (*sakoku*), Japanese subjects residing abroad were banned from returning to Japan. On this provision, historian George Sansom states that, in the early seventeenth century, there were Japanese settlements in most parts of Asia, from Taiwan and Macao to the Moluccas, the Philippines, Borneo, Celebes and Java, Siam, and the Malay Peninsula. With this order, the Tokugawa Shogunate "abandoned" the Japanese who resided in these settlements.

Sakoku is usually understood as one of the feudal policies prohibiting "foreigners" from coming to the Japanese archipelago, except for the Dutch, Chinese, and Koreans. Still, as Sansom suggests, the provision involved something more, that is, prohibition of "the Japanese subjects who have resided abroad" from returning, except for those who lived abroad for less than five years and/or those who were unavoidably detained. Why, in the early seventeenth century, did the Tokugawa Shogunate refuse to welcome the Japanese subjects returning to the Japanese archipelagos? The Shogunate apparently used the length of stay of these subjects outside Japan as the most important indicator of their "alien-ness." Does this mean that the Shogunate used something that we might call "authentic Japanese-ness" to measure the cultural backgrounds of its subjects? Or did the Shogunate understand that, if the Japanese subjects stayed overseas for more than five years, they would surely bring Christianity to home when they return, even though they stayed in non-Christian regions? After all, what made one "the Japanese subject" in the early seventeenth century? Leaving this question to historians, I will proceed to the modern period, and yet, I would like to keep a connection between the seventeenth century and the modern age of empire.

After the end of the isolation policy, Japan began to take a radically different path—the creation and expansion of an empire, incorporating Taiwan, Korea, China, the South Pacific, and Southeast Asia. Indeed, the formation of modern Japan cannot be understood without understanding the nation's endeavor to build, maintain, and expand a large overseas empire. The Japanese state encouraged its people to emigrate to and settle in Japan's overseas empire. To travel to any part of this empire, Japanese emigrants needed no visa for they moved "carrying the [Japanese] state with them."[2] Nevertheless, the gap between those who emigrated to overseas and those who remained in Japan proper was also notable. Let us look at this gap between the Japanese farmers who emigrated to Manchuria to create their "branch villages" and those who had remained in their "mother villages" in Japan.

In the aftermath of the Manchurian Incident of 1931, which induced war fever among Japanese, Manchurian colonization became a state-initiated movement. The Japanese state began to take initiative in Manchurian colonization by first designating thousands of villages in Japan as "special villages for economic rehabilitation" (*keizai kōsei-son*) (Takahashi 1976, 54).[3] Offering grants, subsidies, and other forms of aid, the state asked the village councils to come up with the idea of rehabilitating rural economy that had been hard hit by the Great Depression, fallen price of rice, and natural disasters. Emigration to Manchuria was one, or perhaps the only one, solution. If a large number of farmers would emigrate to Manchuria, "more land" would become available for those who would remain in Japan proper. For this end, the state began a massive campaign. For example, in Nagano prefecture, which was my fieldwork site between 1988 and 1996, the Shinano Overseas Association, which had helped local farmers to emigrate to the United States, Canada, Australia, New Zealand, and South America since 1923, had held "200 lectures and distributed 4,000 books, 15,000 pamphlets, and 350,000 posters promoting Manchurian colonization" (Young 1998, 333). However, Manchurian colonization eventually pitted tenants and small-scale landowners against middle-scale landowners (*chūnō*). That is to say, the village wealthy encouraged poor farmers to emigrate to Manchuria not only to expand the Japanese Empire, but also to mitigate the structural problems of rural Japan, namely, overpopulation, and land shortage. To mobilize as many volunteer-migrants as possible, the village wealthy participated in the fact-finding trips (*shisatsu ryokō*) to Manchuria and brought home their experiences in Manchuria. Yet they hardly returned to Manchuria. In contrast, the poor farmers with little land had no other means but to emigrate to Manchuria in order to rehabilitate their household economy.

Indeed, Manchurian colonization could ease, though only to a small extent, the problems of overpopulation and land shortage at home. For example, the first one hundred farm households, who emigrated from the village of Fujimi in Nagano to Manchuria, had left behind ninety-seven hectare of land (about 19 percent of the cultivated land in the village) and seventy houses (Teikoku Nōkai 1942, 38, 41). The land was then distributed "appropriately among neighborhood cooperatives for communal farm plots" (Young 1998:337; Teikoku Nōkai 1942, 23). In addition, the village council rented out fifty houses to schoolteachers (Teikoku Nōkai, 41). Note, however, that those who had emigrated to Manchuria were excluded from the plan of economic rehabilitation at home. An edict that the Fujimi village council issued to the emigrants to Manchuria reads:

> Those who would return to Fujimi within ten years after their emigration [to Manchuria] shall not enjoy the privileges customarily given to the village residents. If they return, they may have to repay the debts [that they were exempted upon emigrating to Manchuria] and return the subsidies that they received [from the state]. (Teikoku Nōkai, 25)[4]

This edict certainly resonates with the order of the Tokugawa Shogunate issued in the seventeenth century. While middling farmers were expected to create a classless Utopia in Japan proper, tenants and small-scale farmers were expected to build a Utopia in Manchuria. In this respect, emigrants were the victims of economic rehabilitation programs at home.

After Japan's capitulation, however, Japanese colonists had to return home. Since they had carried the state with them when emigrating to Manchuria, they had to return to Japan proper to be under the protection of the same state. *Hikiage*, then, is one of the inevitable consequences of the fall of Japan's empire: having lost the status of the colonizer, Japanese farmers had to return home, often penniless. While they did not experience aerial bombings by the Allied Forces, not to mention of atom bombing, many of them lost their loved ones (and overseas properties) after Japan's capitulation. Nevertheless, the Japanese state, which lost its sovereignty under the U.S. Occupation Forces in 1945, hardly welcomed the returnees from overseas; on August 14, thirty-one and September 24, 1945, the Japanese state issued an order, recommending overseas Japanese to remain in the vanquished empire. The state did not begin accepting overseas Japanese until it finally acknowledged the lawless conditions spreading in China. Still, the Japanese state feared the "germs" that its overseas citizens would bring home from abroad. Thus, upon landing on the Japanese soil (or while they were still on repatriation vessels), the repatriates were repeatedly disinfected with DDT. They were bathed thoroughly and inoculated against diseases such as cholera, typhoid, typhus, small pox, and tetanus (Kōsei-shō 1978, 128–29).[5] In addition, women older than fifteen years of age were encouraged to receive checkups for pregnancy and sexually transmitted diseases at the ports of entry to Japan (ibid, 134). If found pregnant, these women underwent painful abortions without anesthesia: the state assumed that their children, if born *in Japan*, would harm the racial integrity of Japanese people (Kamitsubo 1979, 167–209; Jin'no 1992, 188–91).

My informants, former agrarian colonists in Manchuria, who returned to Nagano between 1946 and 1949, also speak to the fact that they were unwelcome when they managed to return home.[6] At the time of my interview in 1996, Aki described her return to Fujimi as follows: "My neighbors were not kind to us Manchurian daughters (*manshū musume*). I truly worried that I might become an old mistress." "Manchurian daughters" refer to the Japanese women who spent several years of their youth in Manchuria. According to Aki, every arranged marriage failed largely because she was "a returnee from Manchuria." In the end, Aki married a "Manchurian boy" (*manshū otoko*) whom I could not meet since he died a few years earlier before my first stint of fieldwork. Yoshio, another returnee, said: "Once we regained our health, we went out to work as day laborers. Some of us went back to charcoal making. Those women who could find factory work were really lucky. . . . Those who had sent us off with band music [when we left for Manchuria] were not even interested in talking to us." Here, however, we must remember that, in the immediate postwar era, those who had remained in Japan proper also became war victims. Thousands of women had been widowed or were still waiting for the return of their husbands and fathers. Thousands of children were deprived of their parents and homes. While a few made themselves rich through black market operations, most had only limited resources. Hence, the returnees from abroad posed threats upon those who had never left Japan proper. After all, while village governments' edicts were no longer effective, agrarian colonists who had emigrated to Manchuria were not expected to return in the first place—the reason why many returnees from Manchuria were encouraged to settle somewhere else other than their home villages. Indeed, among all the agrarian settlers repatriated to Nagano, as many as 5,810 families gave up their home villages between 1946 and 1955 and moved to other locations within Nagano or other prefectures in Japan (Manshū Kaitaku-shi Kankō-kai 1984a, 736, 741).[7] For example, the village record of Ohinata in Nagano shows that, among 343 repatriates from Manchuria, 164 (or 65 families) eventually left the village and migrated internally to Karuizawa within Nagano prefecture (Manshū Kaitaku-shi Kankō-kai 1984b, 167).

Under these circumstances, the returnees from Japan's fallen empire founded the National Federation of Repatriate Groups (hereafter the NFRG), and soon developed a fierce politics asking for compensation for their lost properties. Such properties included not only the assets that they had built up overseas: they also included the assets that they had given up in Japan upon emigrating to overseas. In the 1960s, however, the NFRG's politics brought the repatriates closer to Japan's postwar conservative government. Following the precedence set by the veterans and bereaved families, the repatriates claimed that their victim experience was exceptionally traumatic. Such an experience, they further claimed, embodies a special service to the nation. Since the repatriates enabled postwar Japan to eventually enjoy "peace and prosperity," they insisted, they should be entitled to receive "special treatments" including honoraria, solatia, and compensation (Orr 2001, 141).

In *The Victim as Hero*, James Orr has painstakingly documented the history of the repatriates' political movement from the immediate postwar period to the late 1960s. According to Orr, beginning in the late 1940s, the Japanese state extended substantial help to the repatriates in order to rebuild their lives, in the form of job training services, counseling centers, or temporary housing. In 1948 and 1949, the Repatriates' Relief Bureau initiated the charity movement "for increasing public sympathy and help for reintegrating repatriates into domestic Japanese society" (Orr 2001, 156–57). Orr reminds us that, from 1945 to the 1960s, "most Japanese felt themselves more or less to be victims of the war." He then calls this national consciousness "the mythologies of Japanese victimhood" (Orr 2001, 139). Instead of questioning the responsibility of each Japanese citizen for the outcome of the war, such mythologies only blamed "militarist others" for the nation's wartime aggression. In other words, the Japanese were the victims of their own state, just like the Chinese and other Asians who were victimized by the Japanese state. An individual Japanese citizen was thus free from accusation by the non-Japanese Asian victims. In this argument, "militarist others" belonged solely to the past, the rhetoric that enabled the repatriates to rely on the postwar, conservative government in their politics of compensation. The amounts of compensations that they received in 1957 and 1967 are small, not comparable with the handsome pensions that the veterans (and the surviving families of fallen soldiers) received.[8] And yet, with their strong ties to the leading political party, the repatriates from the vanquished empire emerged, already in the late 1960s, as a conservative force. The politics of repatriates, then, completely ignored the effects of Japanese aggression on the Chinese people.

Conflict Situations 3 and 2

In her autobiography, Yasui Tomoko, who was repatriated to Japan in 1946, describes her painful journey of escape from Xinjing (Manchukuo's capital) in the aftermath of Japan's capitulation. On her way, Tomoko met a woman, a wife of an agrarian colonist, who told her the following story.

> We [mothers] gathered those children who could no longer walk in one location. With long strings that we managed to find, we tied each child to one big tree. [The strings were long enough so that the children could walk around the tree.] We then scattered candies and crackers around the tree. We prayed for them so that they could at least live for a while during the time of which some, kind [Chinese] people would save them. (Yasui 1972, 64)

In the utter confusion ensuing the Soviet invasion of Manchuria and the subsequent defeat of Japan, Japanese mothers not only tied their children to a tree. They also relinquished their sick children to Chinese couples. Imagine that, if saved by "some kind Chinese people," these children, now adults, must be somewhere in China today. The mothers, if they survived and returned home, shall never forget them, and the children may also remember their mothers if they were old enough in 1945. Note here that Japan and China did not resume diplomatic relations until 1972. Unlike the mothers of these children, the Japanese state opted simply to forget them; in 1959, the Japanese Ministry of Health and Welfare, which had been taking care of affairs of Japanese repatriation since 1945, changed the status of those missing children to "the dead." Even after 1972, the Japanese state did nothing about "the dead" in China. Instead of the state, it is the parents of the missing children who initiated the search for their loved ones. Such a task, however, was often beyond the power of individual citizens. Thus, in 1975, urged by these parents, the state finally entered the search for the missing children of Japanese agrarian colonists in China.

The search for such "children," who were no longer children, identification of them as Japanese, and ultimate repatriation of them to Japan turned out to be long and complicated processes, which I have discussed elsewhere (Tamanoi 2000). The reasons are several. First is the formidable system of nation-states. Second, having separated from their relatives in the aftermath of Japan's capitulation while they were infants or small children, these orphans hardly remember their biological families. Third, during the Cultural Revolution, their Chinese adoptive parents, who raised the children of the former colonizer, tried to withhold their memories for fear of being prosecuted by the Chinese government. Fourth is a language barrier. The orphans have forgotten the Japanese language or have never learned it. Most of their Japanese relatives do not speak

Chinese. When the existence of these Japanese orphans became known in Japan in the 1970s, however, these "state-less" and "culture-less" people fueled "the mythologies of victimhood" in Japan: these poor orphans are the victims of the Japanese state's negligence—the image that Japan's media greatly emphasized.

Here, resigning myself for the moment to the idea that, in the Japanese mass media, we cannot possibly hear the genuine voices of orphans, I will examine a television news program that reported the two-week stay of forty-seven orphans in Japan in 1981. Below is a brief synopsis of this program.

> The program first shows the airplane landing at the Tokyo International Airport with forty-seven orphans on board. It then shows much embracing between these orphans and the officers of the Japanese Ministry of Health and Welfare as well as members of the Japan-China Friendship. Both organizations helped the orphans in realizing their return trips to Japan. Every time when an orphan succeeds in discovering his or her root identity, the program shows an image of a dramatic encounter between an orphan and his or her relatives: they embrace each other and often cry profusely. At the same time, close-up shots of tears on the faces of orphans, who are still unable to prove their identities, are televised. To his great disappointment, one orphan discovers that his parents died several years before his visit. Although he has discovered his root identity, the only thing left for him to do was to visit his family tomb and weep in front of it. The program shows him talking (in Chinese) to his parents, now buried in the tomb, with the following subtitle, "Please forgive this unfaithful son of yours." Lastly, the program airs the scene of a farewell party before their return to China. Once again, the camera shows the tears of orphans, who are still in search of their Japanese names. The camera contrasts them with those happily smiling because they now know their root identities. In a few months, they are to return to Japan finally and permanently.[9]

Between 1972 and 2005, the total of thirty-four groups of orphans who were in search of their identities visited Japan. Each time, then, the media portrayed such a visit of orphans in almost exactly the same manner as the above.

During my fieldwork in Nagano in 1988, I often watched, with a mixture of bemusement and sympathy, these television programs with my neighbors, some of whom were repatriated from Manchuria between

1946 and 1949. In their treatment of orphans, the media was deeply sympathetic, always portraying them as innocent victims who were once powerless children, incapable of making decisions. They "were tossed around by the waves of history (*rekishi ni honrō sareta*)" yet the program hardly explained this history. On the television screen, orphans always looked poor and uneducated, suggesting that these "Japanese" from rural China would never fit in a modern, affluent Japan. After all, they did not speak Japanese, nor did they have a knowledge of Japanese customs. Scenes of the state's employees teaching orphans Japanese songs or "paper folding" (*origami*) surely made them look like children. The state and media's insistence on the continuous use of *orphans* seemed only to reinforce this image on the screen. Nevertheless, the voices of those who have allegedly suffered seem to have altogether been erased from the media's portrayal of them.[10]

In portraying orphans, then, the Japanese media stress the following "facts":

• At the time of Japan's capitulation, the children of Japanese agrarian settlers in Manchuria were helpless small children.

• They grew up in a country that was alien to them.

• They grew up in a poor, rural region of Northeast China.

• They were raised by Chinese adoptive parents. The latter tended to use them as a source of labor.

• Hence, these Japanese children missed the opportunity to learn their mother tongue or have forgotten it.

• They also missed the opportunity to learn Japanese culture or have forgotten it.

• They have suffered from various discriminating practices in China because they are Japanese; their suffering was particularly acute during the Cultural Revolution.

• They have been deprived of the love of their birth parents.

• They lost their fatherland, Japan, and they have been deprived of the universal human right to a nationality [of Japan]. Hence, they are unable to find their place in the system of nation-states.[11]

• As a result of all of the above, they are ignorant of their identities.

If we accept all these "facts" to be valid, there is only one means to redress the suffering of the orphans: by restoring to them Japanese nationality, thereby enabling them to permanently settle in Japan with their Japanese relatives. Predictably, this is the solution to which the Japanese state has adhered since 1981 without, apparently, listening to the genuine voices of orphans.

Can we, then, listen to the orphans' voices? In 1998, with the help of Mrs. Sakurai, I recorded the following narratives of two orphans in Tokyo, whom I call Mr. Suzuki and Mr. Kobayashi respectively. Mrs. Sakurai was then teaching Japanese to these orphans. Since both Mr. Suzuki and Mr. Kobayashi spoke in Chinese, she translated their stories for me. Below are the summaries of these two orphans' narratives.

Mr. Suzuki: I was about two when I was separated from my family, so I hardly remember what happened then. Many years later, I found out that my father had died soon after his arrival in Manchuria. [After Japan's capitulation] I was dying of malnutrition and so my mother entrusted me to my adoptive parents in exchange for food. My adoptive parents did not have children of their own. They were very poor and made me work once I regained my health. But they let me attend a school when I was about seven. When I was eleven or so, my adoptive father died. My adoptive mother remarried, but my second adoptive father died soon after in 1961. I knew I was Japanese since I was seven because the kids at my school called me "a little Japanese" all the time. However hard I pressed my adoptive mother, she did not tell me anything about my parents. In 1960, I married a Chinese woman, and we later had four sons and one daughter. A few years after 1972, two Japanese women in the village where I lived returned temporarily to Japan. They were sisters, and older than I was. While in Japan, these two sisters received a visit from my mother and elder sister. I wanted to return to Japan badly, but my adoptive mother pleaded with me not to leave her. In the end, I waited until she passed away. That was 1988. The following year, I returned to Japan with my wife and fourth son. My mother lives in Wakayama with my sister and her family. She also has three sons, all of whom are married. They were all good to us, but we decided to move out of my mother's house to Yokohama. We did not want to be dependent on them, and this way, I was able to find a job.

Mr. Kobayashi: What I will tell you is what I later learned. I was about four when Japan surrendered. I am a survivor of the compulsory group suicide that took place in the colony of Hataho.

My mother, my two brothers, and another sister all died in this collective suicide. As my father had been drafted, he was then not with us. My elder sister and I survived this ordeal. Later, a Chinese man approached me and took me to his home, while someone else took my sister to his home. My adoptive parents were poor. I remember they had five or six children of their own but the children died one after another, except for one daughter. I guess they needed a boy. I worked very hard. When I first went to school, I was already ten years old. I knew I was Japanese. My friends called me "a little Japanese" and often ridiculed me. In 1960, I married a Chinese woman and we had two daughters and one son. Soon after, I met a Japanese woman who was able to speak and write Japanese. [After 1972] I wrote many letters and asked the Japanese government to search for my relatives in Japan. When, in 1980, a group of Japanese visited our village to pay their respects to Japanese who had died there, I asked them to search for my relatives. In 1982, to my great surprise, I received a letter from my father. He had remarried, to a woman who had lost her husband in Manchuria. She already had three children from her previous marriage. Later, my father had two more boys with her. I visited my father for a short while in 1982 and told him that I would like to return to Japan, but his wife, that is, my stepmother, adamantly opposed my return. My father told me that I would have nothing to inherit from him. I guess it was his wife who made him say this. But after 1982, both my father and stepmother died. Finally, in 1986, I returned with my wife and three children to Hiratsuka. My children quickly learned Japanese and now have good jobs. But they have left home. I worked at a small factory for more than ten years, and we now live on my small pensions. My wife is still able to work. When she stops working, I wonder whether we may have to ask the government for livelihood assistance.

The narratives of Mr. Suzuki and Mr. Kobayashi reveal several common elements of the life histories of orphans who have returned to Japan. First, they have many "families," but each of these families suffer(ed) from the inevitable forces originating in the system of nation-states. The families to which they were born were shattered in the aftermath of the Soviet invasion of Manchuria and Japan's capitulation. While the situations of families into which they had been adopted varied greatly, the adoptive families were, generally speaking, poor. Thus, in postwar Japan, two, mutually opposing, images of the adoptive parents coexist:

benevolent parents who sacrificed their own lives to raise their Japanese children, and abusive parents who exploited the children's labor for their own survival. Both are media creations and are, perhaps, untrue. And yet, both Mr. Suzuki and Mr. Kobayashi tell us, even though most adoptive parents were poor and some were abusive, they "saved our lives and made us live," for which they are grateful. Lastly, the families raised by the orphans in China also suffer(ed) from the inevitable forces originating in the system of nation-states. When the orphans decided to return to Japan, some of their family members opposed the idea of going to Japan. While Mr. Kobayashi returned with his entire family, Mr. Suzuki returned only with his wife and fourth son. For some orphans, then, returning home meant severing ties with some of their Chinese relatives. When this happens, it is usually the adoptive parents who suffered most, not only a financial loss but also an incalculable social loss. In addition, the Japanese state closely monitors which orphans are entitled to return to Japan, and which members of their families are able to return with them.[12]

Second, while in China, these orphans were on the margin of Chinese society. Once they return to Japan, they are on the margin of Japanese society. Indeed, for quite some time after 1972, the Japanese state regarded them as "aliens." Even though some were able to locate their family registers (koseki) where their names are recorded in Japanese, they still had to carry "certificates of alien status" (gaikokujin tōrokushō) while in Japan. Hence, for orphans, restoring a Japanese nationality has become first on the list of things to do after they return to Japan. However, Japanese-Chinese children and grandchildren of these orphans do not necessarily wish to become naturalized Japanese. In these cases, the orphans (who must prove their Japanese nationality) and their family members must live with two distinct nationalities in Japan, which does not allow its citizens to hold double nationalities. After all, "Japan is a big family." Consequently, orphans and their families must struggle with the system of nation-states whether they are in China or in Japan, and repatriation to Japan in itself hardly ameliorates their struggle.

As I have already discussed, those who initiated the search for orphans are the repatriates who lost their family members, friends, and neighbors in Manchuria in the aftermath of Japan's capitulation. While the Japanese state joined them later in searching for orphans, once joined, the state needed these repatriates as "volunteers" who would assist orphans so the latter were able to settle in Japan permanently. In both Nagano and Tokyo (where I began my fieldwork in 1998), these volunteers welcomed orphans who visited Japan for the first time. They also accompanied orphans throughout their stay in Japan and assisted them in their search for Japanese relatives. Once these orphans returned to Japan permanently, these volunteers offered them a variety of assistance. They taught orphans how to shop at a grocery store, how to install a home telephone, and how to open a bank account. They accompanied orphans to the city halls so that these Japanese who were unable to speak Japanese could restore Japanese nationality or newly obtain ones for their Chinese spouses and Japanese-Chinese children. When these orphans applied for welfare programs, the same volunteers helped them to fill in complicated documents. The orphans desperately needed these supervisions because most of them eventually chose to live by themselves in large towns, rather than living with their Japanese relatives in rural areas. The volunteers, who spent a considerable amount of time with orphans, were thus able to listen to the genuine voices of orphans. At the same time, however, these volunteers had to act as the Japanese state's agents, endorsing the state's policy, that is, to offer the orphans Japanese nationality (if they prove their Japanese identities) and make them return permanently to Japan. But if orphans choose not to regain Japanese nationality, what would these volunteers do? If orphans choose to stay in China with their Chinese adoptive parents, do the volunteers refuse to help them? How do they approach the children and grandchildren of orphans, who want to keep their Chinese nationality but who visit Japan anyway for merely economic reasons? Herein, then, lie the seeds of conflict situations.

In 1998, I met Mr. Takahashi in Tokyo, a volunteer and himself a repatriate from Manchuria, who was then assisting orphans as they tried to settle in Japan permanently. At the time of my interview, he told me the following: "These days, it is hard to tell who is 'Japanese' and who is 'Chinese.' How can you tell the difference between *zanryū koji* [and their family members] and those [Chinese] smuggling into Japan from Fujian province?" The Chinese from Fujian province are believed to have a "centuries-old tradition of going overseas to make a fortune" (Nonini and Ong 1997, 3). Indeed, Chinese from Fujian province emigrated in mass to Manchuria in the age of empire. There they became a source of irritation for the Japanese colonial authorities. Today, they are immigrating again, not to Manchuria but to Japan. These immigrants are apparently irritating not only Mr. Takahashi, but also the Japanese public at large. According to the Japanese media reports, these Chinese try to enter Japan illegally and, to that end, turn to the smuggling syndicates with connections not only in Japan, but also in Taiwan, Hong Kong, Southeast Asia, and even Central and South America. Yet, the following case illustrates the difficulty of distinguishing (Japanese) orphans from the Chinese illegal immigrants.

In 1997, a woman, who was later identified as Chinese, was "repatriated" to Japan. The Japanese government, which had earlier identified her as a child of Japanese agrarian settlers in Manchuria, paid for her trip to Japan and her initial stay in Tokyo. Once the woman arrived in Tokyo, however, it did not take long for the Japanese authority to prove the falsification of her identity. She was immediately deported back to China. In this case, the woman paid an immigration broker to falsify the record in her passport. Interestingly, this immigration broker himself was a son of another orphan repatriated to Japan a couple of years earlier.[13] Reporting on this and other similar incidents, the Japanese media soon coined the term *nise koji*, "false orphans." Deifying and utilizing the nation-state system, false orphans have tried to enter Japan at their own risk.

False orphans, then, are part of the Chinese immigrants to Japan in the age of global capitalism. Such illegal immigrants are often called *gisō nan'min*, "false refugees," another term coined by the media in the mid-1990s. Having been smuggled into Japan by immigration brokers, false refugees carry few, if any, personal belongings when they enter the country. Hence, their appearance as refugees. The Japanese government rarely accept applications for refugee or asylum status. Thus, however much they resemble refugees, false refugees are considered illegal immigrants. [14] According to statistics provided by the Immigration Bureau of Japan, the number of Chinese from the People's Republic of China who held "the certificate of alien status" in 2003 was 462, 396. This number represents about 24 percent of the total number of "aliens" in Japan in the same year. In addition to these legal aliens, however, 29, 676 Chinese stayed illegally in Japan in 2003. Since the mid-1960s, then, the number of Chinese immigrants has increased about ten times. Those foreigners who have the certificate of alien status tend to stay in Japan for a longer period of time, in comparison to, say, tourists. Still, most Chinese immigrants have no intention of staying in Japan permanently. Rather, they enter Japan for the purpose of "studying abroad" or "professional training." When their terms (as students or trainees) are over, however, they tend to stay in Japan on expired visas for economic reasons: to send money back to their homes in China. That is to say, these Chinese are mostly transients, moving back and forth between Japan and China.[15]

Ironically, the arrival of false orphans and false refugees to Japan has caused an unexpected repercussion in the lives of orphans, namely, resurgence of the colonial racism based on the notion of Japanese racial supremacy. It is not that racism began to appear anew once a large number of Chinese unskilled laborers reached Japan in the 1990s. The life of orphans in Japan has always been difficult, and a variety of discriminatory practices against them are partly to be blamed. "The only job I got is a cleaning woman of train cars. I guess this is all right as I do not have to speak [Japanese]," said Mrs. Tanaka, an orphan who returned to Nagano from Northeast China in the early 1980s. However, until the early 1990s, the Japanese media had always described orphans as innocent victims with tremendous sympathy because they were then powerless children, incapable of making decisions. In contrast, since the late 1990s, the media's portrayal of orphans and their spouses and children seems to have drastically changed. For example, the media often reports on the "mental instability" among orphans and points to the tendency among the children of orphans to fail in schoolwork, commit petty crimes, or join gangs. Several newspaper articles have reported that it is the children of orphans who, out of their own greed, try to persuade the parents to return to Japan when the latter have no desire to do so. For example, in 1999, a sixty-year-old orphan killed his son-in-law with the help of his wife and daughter. He confessed to the police that the victim, who is a Chinese citizen, married his daughter only because he wished to emigrate to Japan. Once in Japan, this orphan is reported to have told his lawyer that his son-in-law sent all the money he earned back to his parents in China, without contributing a penny to his marriage family.[16]

This radical transformation of the media-created images of orphans is not unrelated to the sharp increase in numbers of orphans and their families who returned to Japan permanently. The statistics shows that in 2005, the number of orphans who had settled in Japan reached 9,111. This number does not include these orphans' family members and yet, despite the restrictions imposed by the Japanese state on the repatriation of orphans, the returning orphans have been inviting their relatives in China to join them in Japan. To this large group of Japanese nationals, who were raised by Chinese adoptive parents, we must include those Japanese women who, in the aftermath of Japan's capitulation, married Chinese citizens; since 1993, these women have also been returning to Japan permanently. In 2005, their number reached over eleven thousand. Like orphans, these women have been inviting their children and grandchildren who move to Japan from China with their families.[17] In the perception of the mainstream Japanese society, then, the people called "orphans" are no longer the tragic victims of Japanese imperialism. Rather, they are the ones who bring Chinese or half-Chinese people to Japan. They therefore can potentially threaten the "integrity" of the family called "Japan." Put differently, in the eyes of Japanese public, the difference between orphans and their family members on the one hand, and Chinese illegal immigrants on the other, has become extremely thin.

Discussion and Conclusion

Writing on children growing up in an era of global capitalism, Sharon Stephens asks a series of poignant questions:

> What sorts of social visions and notions of culture underlie assertions within international-rights discourses that every child has a right to a cultural identity? To what extent is this identity conceived as singular and exclusive, and what sorts of priorities are asserted in cases where various forms of cultural identity— regional, national, ethnic minority, or indigenous—come up against one another? (Stephens 1995, 3)

Stephens is interested in the "complex globalizations of the once localized Western constructions of childhood," and the impact on those constructions on the everyday lives of children in the contemporary world (Stephens, 8; see also Schaeper-Hughes and Sargent 1998). Here, overlapping the orphans and their children with the children growing up in a multicultural setting, I argue that the orphans and their family members have a right not to be constrained within an exclusionary Japanese cultural identity and "not to have their bodies and minds appropriated as the unprotected terrain upon which cultural battles are fought" (Stephens 1995, 4). In the case of orphans and their children, "cultural battles" are complex, and are often imposed on them. Furthermore, such battles have been taking place largely in their absence, among the Japanese government, media, society at large, and those who returned from Manchuria soon after Japan's capitulation. Unless the latter find many more ways to communicate with the orphans, there is a serious danger in that orphans and their children will be consumed in these cultural battles, their voices left unheard. Thus, in concluding this chapter, I will depict some ethnographic scenes in which both orphans and their Japanese relatives (who now work as volunteers for orphans) act as independent agents, rather than the pawns of the Japanese state and/or media.

In 2001, on the day of the anniversary of the end of the war, near the Tokyo Station, I witnessed about six hundred people quietly marching from the station building to the busy commercial district of Ginza through Hibiya Park.[18] They were not young; they seemed to vary in age from fifty to seventy. Some were holding white and yellow banners with messages reading: We are the orphans from China; Assure our post retirement life; and Please do not forget us. The protesters were evidently orphans who were recently repatriated from China. I then remembered Mr. Takahashi's words: even if an orphan worked for ten years after repatriation to Japan, after retirement, he or she would only be eligible for a monthly annuity of about 50,000 yen or about $440. Because this is by no means enough to live on, such retirees inevitably receive welfare assistance, inviting criticism from the Japanese public. However, welfare assistance restricts the life of orphans in many ways. If an orphan returns to China to spend several weeks to take care of his or her adoptive parents, he or she is not entitled to receive welfare money during those weeks. If an orphan buys a television, the employees of the welfare office would ask how come he or she is able to buy such a luxury item. Thus, in this march, orphans protested the Japanese government that had offered them a Japanese nationality but not a full Japanese citizenship.

The following year, this group of orphans went far beyond staging a protest march, bringing a lawsuit before the Tokyo Metropolitan Circuit Court against the Japanese government. The plaintiffs, numbering 637, claimed the following. First, the Japanese state deserted them in Manchuria after the demise of the Japanese Empire. Second, in 1959, the Japanese state changed the status of "the missing" to "the dead" in the Japanese household registries without due investigation. Third, since repatriation, the Japanese state has not provided the orphans with the adequate assistance. Therefore, each plaintiff claims compensation from the Japanese state for his or her ruined life in the amount of 33 million yen or about $300,000.[19] In this lawsuit, which has not yet concluded, the orphans question the gap between the Japanese nationality (that they have) and the Japanese citizenship (that they believe they do not have). Restated, they have transformed the gift from the Japanese state—Japanese nationality—into a vehicle for demanding full Japanese citizenship.[20] In this lawsuit as well as the protest march, orphans have been greatly helped by people like Mr. Takahashi, the colonists in Manchuria who returned to Japan soon after Japan's capitulation. These volunteers have become one collective *Japanese* "parent" to the orphans.

While the above incidents present orphans as active agents, the following narratives present the orphans' children as active agents. In 1998, Mr. Takahashi introduced me to Mr. Wang, who told me the following: "I do not care whether my father is Japanese or not. He made me retain my Chinese nationality, but my brother has obtained Japanese nationality. This is good for us as we are planning to start a taxi company in China in the near future after we earn enough money here in Japan." Mr. Wang's father is a child of Japanese agrarian colonists in Manchuria. Although he was able to prove his root identity, Mr. Wang has never met the Japanese relatives of his father. Although he returned to Japan at the Japanese government's expense, he has retained his Chinese name and nationality (because, he said, "my father does not remember his Japanese name anyway"). Mr. Wang's father lives on pensions, but he has been leading a busy life in Tokyo with his brother. Once an elementary school teacher in Northeast China, he now works in Japan six days a week, thirteen hours a day, in a small factory. After China joined the World Trade Organization, many family members of orphans apparently opted to keep their Chinese nationality. Instead of permanently returning to Japan, they combine, within their extended families, the Japanese and Chinese nationalities to achieve various economic goals. Mr. Wang's story suggests the emergence of the orphans' children who could play with "flexible citizenship," and who make the best out of the often adversarial circumstances.[21]

Those who joined the protest march and the lawsuit against the Japanese state, and such people as Mr. Wang, then, have finally stood up in front of the Japanese public and begun to speak. Nevertheless, there is an unavoidable gap between these two parties. That is, those who joined the protest march and the lawsuit demand that they be treated as the full citizens of Japan. In contrast, Mr. Wang would like to move freely between China and Japan. For that end, he would like to keep the dual nationalities within his extended family. Both stand on the edge of the Japanese society. However, while one desperately tries to be "Japanese," another chooses not to be.

Here, let me return to the story of Ichirō and several questions I asked about him at the onset of this chapter. If Ichirō remains to be Japanese, conflicts will not emerge between him and his fans in Japan. But if he chooses to be a U.S. citizen, what will happen to his Japanese fans? Why does a change of citizenship alter the personality of an individual such as Ichirō in the eyes of the Japanese audience? Likewise, as long as the orphans and their children speak and act as Japanese, conflicts between them and the Japanese volunteers who help their permanent settlements in Japan may be more subtle. But what if the orphans and their children choose to remain Chinese, can the Japanese volunteers still accept them as their children? The answer to this question seems to depend on yet another question, which has to be answered affirmatively. That is, are the Japanese volunteers and the Japanese public willing to make efforts to listen to the genuine voices of orphans and their families? At the same time, we should remember that, at the edge of Japan (and China), conflicts have always been part of the routine stories of many families since, most probably, the seventeenth century. In this sense, those who stand at the edge of the Japanese archipelagos, whether they may be Ichirō or the descendants of Japanese agrarian colonists in Manchuria, are not the sources of conflicts. Rather, such sources always lie among those who are firmly situated in the center of the same archipelagos.

Notes

Is "Japan" Still A Big Family?

1. The Japanese state defines *zanryū koji* in the following: First, they were born of the Japanese parents of mostly agrarian colonists, either in Japan or Manchuria. Second, they were orphaned or separated from their families in the wake of the Soviet invasion of Manchuria and Japan's capitulation. *Zanryū koji* were younger than thirteen, and were soon placed, usually by the will of their parents, in Chinese families. For this reason, they have Chinese names and a Chinese nationality. They are therefore unsure of their *mimoto*, a highly primordial notion that literally means "the roots of a person's body." In other words, they do not know who they are. In 1993, however, the state was forced to create another category called *zanryū fujin*, "the women who have remained behind (in China)." This term refers to the Japanese women, who were older than thirteen at the time of Japan's capitulation, and who later married the Chinese citizens. Having believed, erroneously, that these women chose their life courses out of their own will, the state denied any assistance to *zanryū fujin* until 1993.

2. This phrase originates in the book written by a British imperial historian, J. R. Seeley (1883). It often appeared in the Japanese intellectual discourses during the age of empire.

3. Between 1932 and 1936, the Japanese state designated the total of 6,559 villages and towns to be "special villages for economic regeneration" (see Nōson Kōsei Kyōkai 1937).

4. The Village Councils of both Ohinata and Hirane issued the same edicts to the emigrants to Manchuria (Nōson Kōsei Kyōkai 1937, 26).

5. For more detailed records of the Japanese government's battle with diseases and epidemics rampant among repatriates, see *Hikiage ken'eki-shi* [The History of the Quarantine for the Repatriates] (Kōsei-shō 1947, 1948). This three-volume book presents the meticulous records of the day-to-day battle of the officers at the Japanese Ministry of Health in taming the epidemics at the ports of entry into Japan between 1945 and 1947.

6. In 1984, I visited southern Nagano for another research topic that is only fractionally related to the topic of this chapter. Little did I know then that Nagano sent approximately thirty-seven thousand agrarian colonists to Manchuria in the 1930s and 1940s (Young 1998, 329). Thus, as my fieldwork progressed, I met an increasing number of the repatriates from Manchuria in the same general area. In 1988, I stayed in southern Nagano for the duration of a year to complete my original research. Then, shifting my research topic to the Japanese colonization of Manchuria, I returned to the same area beginning in 1989, each time staying there for about a month.

7. In *Kyū manshū kaitaku-dan no sengo* [The Postwar Conditions of the Former Agrarian Colonists in Manchuria], Wada Noboru chronicles one such family of repatriates who emigrated to Karuizawa in the immediate postwar era. The Sakamoto family emigrated to Manchuria from the Village of Ohinata. After

repatriation, they moved to Karuizawa together with several other families. When Father Conrad, who was a missionary in China before the war, moved to Japan in the early 1950s and built a Catholic Church near their settlement, all in the Sakamoto family converted to Catholicism. While their religious conversion can be interpreted in many ways, it at least suggests the harsh reality that the repatriates faced in postwar Japan. Later on, when the wave of economic development reached the area, many abandoned farming, sold land to developers and moved to other locations in Japan (1993).

8. In 1957, the Japanese state granted only from 7,000 yen to those repatriates who were under thirty (but older than eight) at the war's end to 28,000 yen to those who were over fifty (Jin'no 1992, 198–99). Families of those who died while awaiting repatriation also received comparable payments. However, those who had succeeded in rebuilding their livelihoods in postwar Japan were excluded from the benefits. In 1962, demands for compensations picked up again "when the statue of limitation on debts threatened to nullify lost assets claims on the government" (Orr 2001, 161). Finally, in 1967, appreciating "their troubles," the Japanese state installed another round of payments, 192.5 billion *yen* to be distributed among the repatriates. While those who were over fifty at the time of Japan's capitulation received 160,000 *yen*, those who were younger than twenty received 20,000 *yen* (Jin'no 1992, 199). This time, to determine the amount of compensation, the income level of the repatriates was not taken into account. Instead, the state sanctified the repatriates' suffering as service to the state. The repatriates in turn dropped "their open disparagement of the wartime government continental expansion policy and put a positive spin on their cooperation with that policy" (Orr 2001, 165–66).

9. "Nihon Hōsō Kyōkai (Japan National Broadcasting Station) News Highlights," 1981.

10. This is also the case with the print media. Such books as *Manshū kimin* [The Abandoned People in Manchuria] (Mitome, 1988) or *Manshū, sono maboroshi no kuni yue ni* [Manchuria, the Country of Illusion] (Hayashi, 1986) were written by the journalists who were born in Japan many years after 1945. In these books, orphans do not speak: they are spoken for. So much so that one book, which was indeed written by two orphans, was published with the following title: *Nitchū no hazama ni ikite: jibun de kaita zanryū koji no kiroku* [Having Lived in between Japan and China: Records Genuinely Written by Zanryū Koji] Daidō and Suzuki, 1988). Yet, even this book is not free from the bias of the editor who translated orphans' essays to Japanese.

11. For this argument, the media often rely on Article 15 of the Universal Declaration of Human Rights, which states: "Everyone has the right to a nationality. No one shall be arbitrarily deprived of his nationality nor denied the right to change his nationality."

12. Until 1992, the adult (older than twenty years of age) or married children of orphans were not allowed to return to Japan with their parents on the government's expenses. In that year, the government implemented the policy that allowed a "disabled" orphan to return with one of his or her children. Two

years later, the government began to apply the same policy to any orphan older than sixty-five-years-old. In 1995, the government lowered the age threshold to sixty (Kōsei-shō 1997, 419).

13. There are many articles reporting on this incident and several other cases of "false orphans." See, for example, *Asahi*, January 6, April 15, June 2, June 5, 1998; and *Yomiuri*, December 16, 1997, May 11, June 1, August 1, 1998.

14. Since 1990, Japan has accepted only *Nikkei* as unskilled or semiskilled laborers. Here, *Nikkei* refers to the approximately two hundred thousand descendants of Japanese immigrants to Latin America. In 1990, the immigration law was revised, primarily because the then vibrant Japanese economy was suffering from a labor shortage. The *Nikkei* population thus responded to "an explosive demand for labor in manufacturing industries in jobs shunned by Japanese" (Yamanaka 1996, 65; see also Tsuda 2003).

15. See "Gaikokujin no nyūkoku jyōkyō" [Statistics on the entry of foreigners into Japan) and "Honpō ni okeru fuhō zanryūsha sū ni tsuite" [Concerning visa overstayers in Japan) at the home page of the Japanese Ministry of Justice, http://www.moj.go.jp.

16. Both incidents are reported in the following newspapers. *Yomiuri*, December 16, 1997, June 1, 1998, and *Asahi*, December 7, 1999.

17. See *Tongsheng tonqi* [Same voice, same people], available from http://www.kikokusha-center.or.jp, accessed October 16, 2006. This is the official name of the site created by Chūgoku Kikokusha Teichaku Sokushin Sentā (Center for Returnees from China) located in Tokorozawa, Saitama prefecture, Japan (see also Ōkubo 2004, 222).

18. *Asahi*, evening version, August 15, 2001.

19. *Asahi*, December 20, 2002.

20. Since 2001, more orphans joined this lawsuit in various locations, including Kagoshima, Tokushima, Kōchi, Sapporo, and Osaka. As of 2004, more than half of orphans who have returned to Japan are believed to have become plaintiffs against the Japanese state.

21. Flexible citizenship refers to "the strategies and effects of mobile managers, technocrats, and professionals seeking to both circumvent and benefit from different nation-state regimes by selecting different sites for investments, work, and family locations" (Ong 2002, 174). In Britain, for example, a recent change in immigration policy granted full citizenship to fifty thousand elite Hong Kong Chinese. "The members of this special subcategory of Chinese," A. Ong states, "were carefully chosen from among householders (presumably predominantly male) who had connections in British government, business, or some other organizations" (Ong, 180). These Hong Kong Chinese can enjoy flexible citizenship not just in Britain but in any country they choose, obtaining citizenship by a variety of means, including purchase. And yet, Ong points to "premodern forms of child, gender, and class oppression" that these affluent Hong Kong Chinese have inadvertently created in many parts of the world (Ong, 190). They drop their children, so-called parachute kids, anywhere in the world at will. They leave their wives with their children while they travel freely and extensively. Furthermore, affluent Hong Kong Chinese with flexible citizenship often employ

illegal Chinese immigrants in their factories at low wages. These employees, as well as the children and the wives of the Hong Kong Chinese, are the victims of class, child, or gender repression. In other words, behind those who can resort to flexible citizenship are many people who suffer because of it.

Chapter 7

Someone's Old, Something's New, Someone's Borrowed, Someone's Blue:

Changing Elder Care at the Turn of the 21st Century

Susan Orpett Long

At the beginning of the twenty-first century, advanced industrial societies shared the demographic realities of small families and long life expectancies. People were having fewer children and living longer than ever before, creating populations in which a much larger proportion of people are in older age cohorts. (See figure 7.1.) Since pensions, medical systems, and social welfare programs were established in an earlier demographic era, governments have had to face the challenges of increased demand on these systems from a greatly expanded number of people eligible for payments and services.

In Japan, as in other industrial countries, older citizens are largely active, self-sufficient people. Yet advanced age also means increased potential for illness, frailty, and dependency. In the early part of the twentieth century, life expectancy in Japan was only in the mid-forties. The official family system, created by the government and based on upper-class patterns of the previous Tokugawa period, was expected to provide support and care to household members who did reach old age. In that family system, the oldest son (or alternate heir) succeeded his father as household head and had responsibility for household continuity and the care of all of its members, including his elderly parents. However, the gendered division of labor within the household and in society more broadly allocated the day-to-day tasks of nurturing and bodily care to women,

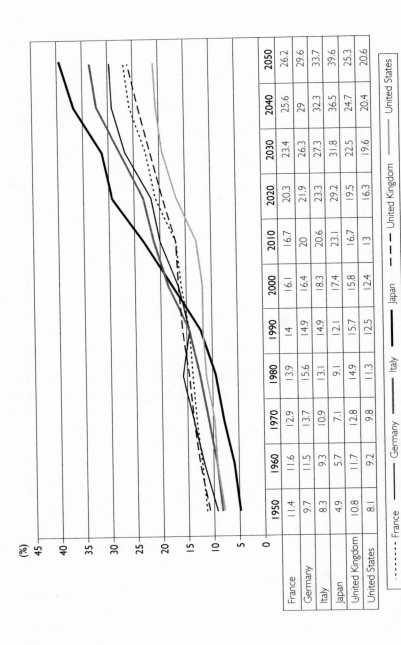

	1950	1960	1970	1980	1990	2000	2010	2020	2030	2040	2050
France	11.4	11.6	12.9	13.9	14	16.1	16.7	20.3	23.4	25.6	26.2
Germany	9.7	11.5	13.7	15.6	14.9	16.4	20	21.9	26.3	29	29.6
Italy	8.3	9.3	10.9	13.1	14.9	18.3	20.6	23.3	27.3	32.3	33.7
Japan	4.9	5.7	7.1	9.1	12.1	17.4	23.1	29.2	31.8	36.5	39.6
United Kingdom	10.8	11.7	12.8	14.9	15.7	15.8	16.7	19.5	22.5	24.7	25.3
United States	8.1	9.2	9.8	11.3	12.5	12.4	13	16.3	19.6	20.4	20.6

······· France ——— Germany ——— Italy ——— Japan – – – United Kingdom ——— United States

Source: OECD Factbook 2007: *Economic, Environmental and Social Statistics*

Figure 7.1 Proportion of People 65 Years and Older in Total Population in Selected Advanced Industrial Countries

so that in reality the wife of the head of household actually performed the work of caregiving. A minimal welfare system was the undesirable alternative for those with no family to provide such support.

However, that was an era in which only about 5 percent of the population was elderly. In the late twentieth century, Japanese policy makers have attempted to find ways to adjust pension, medical, and social welfare systems to respond to increased demand of larger numbers of elderly members of their society. In part, they were reacting to changes in the family that had already taken place, changes that meant that families could no longer handle elder care on their own: fewer children, less likelihood of the elderly living with younger generations of the family, and increases in chronic illnesses of old age once infectious diseases were brought under control through improved public health and affluence in the decades after World War II.

In addition, the Allied Occupation (1945–1952) eliminated the legal structure of family elder care when it established a new family code based on a nuclear family model and on equality of birth order and gender. By the end of the century, presumed daughter-in-law caregivers of the past were likely to be better educated and working away from home in comparison to earlier generations of women. The preference of many women to work in noncareer jobs with lower pay and fewer benefits made them valuable employees in an era of global economic competition. Thus, in the late twentieth century policy makers explored models of extra-familial caregiving for the elderly, studying in particular Scandanavian systems of social welfare and German insurance programs. The programs in place at the beginning of the twenty-first century, including the long-term care insurance system that this chapter describes, are political compromises that are at once Japanese and in the forefront of international social policy. "Tradition" is both challenged and consciously utilized as new ways are adapted to the local context.[1] In an era of rapid change, families and individuals also must adjust, compromise, and search for new solutions that incorporate the old and the new. In regard to succession and inheritance, Keith Brown argued that families are not only structures or cycles, but rather real people doing the best they can to deal with the realities with which demography and history have presented them (Brown 1966). With elder care, too, we must describe not only the way the system is supposed to work, but also the demographic constraints and ways that people creatively respond to their circumstances by mixing solutions to meet their needs.

The title of this chapter alters a bit the old charge to brides, "something old, something new, something borrowed, something blue." In this paper, "someone's old" refers to the "someone" in so many Japanese families who is not just past the official "sixty-five" marker, but who becomes classified as old because of behavior, attitude, and/or disability that leads to dependence on others for meeting basic needs. "Something's new" is the long-term care insurance system that was created as a policy response to the perceived need to create alternatives to reliance on family care in the twenty-first century. Yet insurance can at best *pay* for care; it does not itself provide care. With normative caregivers, that is the wives of the eldest sons, less willing and less available, "someone's borrowed" from other roles. Family caregivers are increasingly husbands, sons, daughters, and wives of younger sons. Borrowing people from nonnormative categories of kin may not be sufficient, and shared caregiving and paid care providers are more and more part of the picture of elder care in Japan. Finally, "someone's blue" points out that the creation of new solutions is not simply a matter of changing policy or of replacing one cultural pattern with another, but is often the source of great stress and pain for the on-the-ground real people. The elderly Japanese and their family caregivers this chapter describes are real people who have told their stories to me or my colleagues in interviews conducted between 1996 and 2004.[2]

Someone's Old

In 2006, life expectancy in Japan was 85.8 years for women and 79.4 years for men. Combined with a completed fertility rate of 1.26, the proportion of elderly in the population is expected to continue to increase from the 2005 figure of 20.1 percent. Perhaps we get a better sense of the need for care, however, from the figure released for "Respect for the Aged Day" in 2007: thirty-two thousand people in Japan are 100 years or older. This number more than tripled from the mid-1990s when it was "only" about ten thousand.

The ratio of elderly people to the entire population and the large number of "old old" suggest that having an elderly relative who needs help in some aspects of his or her life is a common experience. Although the number of households in which an older person lives alone has grown dramatically in recent years, still nearly half of people sixty-five and older live with an adult child.[3] Regardless of the use of outside services, it is these relatives who form the first line of duty in caring for people who cannot manage totally on their own.

Something's New

What is new as of 2000 is a long-term care insurance system (*kaigo hoken seido*), designed to substitute for or supplement family caregiving for ill and frail older people. Having one middle-aged couple needing to care for four elderly, frail or ill parents is a difficult enough proposition by American meanings of caregiving. By Japanese standards it is impossible, since ideal nurturing requires the continuous physical presence of the caregiver, maintaining a calm, positive atmosphere, and making caregiving the sole caregiver's primary role (Long 1997). Thus, it is impossible to be the family caregiver of, for example, a mother and a mother-in-law at the same time, as one woman commented with a sigh: "When my mother needed care, my mother-in-law said, 'That's ok. I'll go to a nursing home.' "

The demographics mean fewer potential caregivers relative to the number who need care. In addition, numerous social changes have limited availability of those previously assumed to be the designated caregiver if help was needed. In particular, the increased participation of women in the labor force[4] and increased geographical mobility have meant that daughters-in-law may have more difficulty taking on the caregiver role. The increased nuclearization of the family in the last half of the twentieth century—not only by numbers, but also by changed expectations, inheritance patterns, and ideals as described by K. Morioka (1984)—have led to behavioral resistance on the part of daughters-in-law who were previously thought to be the "natural" caregiver for their husband's parents. As illustrated by J. Traphagan (2003) and B. R. Jenike (2003), caregiving arrangements have become the subject of negotiation before and during marriage, and the cause of divorce, relocation, and anger.

In the 1980s, Japanese bureaucrats shifted the definition of the issue from "the problems old people have" to "old people as a social problem," that is the problem of the aging society (Campbell 2000). Their response was the creation of the Gold Plan, and later a revised Gold Plan, which set out goals for the development of institutional and community-based care services. After years of studying European and American systems of elder care and of political debate in the 1990s, it was decided to supplement the Gold Plan which relied fully on tax money for funding and on local governments to administer. Rather than being motivated to solve the problems of the elderly, politicians, according to Paul Talcott (2002), were looking for votes from the increasingly large proportion of the population of senior citizens. Although the system they created was based on a similar insurance approach put into place in Germany several years previously, the Japanese long-term care program covers more people and is more generous in its benefits than its German model. The Japanese long-term care system is a mandatory insurance program in which everyone over forty years old pays insurance premiums, and everyone over sixty-five and/or suffering from a "disease of aging" is guaranteed certain services according only to their biological and social needs and *not* to their ability to pay. The benefits are paid only in the form of services and equipment, and not in cash. The cost of the program is born equally by the insurance fund (that is, premiums) and a combination of national and local tax monies. The guarantee of services has created strong demand that encourages development of service-providing organizations. It has resulted in a tremendous expansion of programs and facilities for the elderly, which are owned by nonprofit groups, entrepreneurs, and large corporations.

The elderly person, or someone on his or her behalf, applies at the local government office, which generates an assessment of problems in daily living by a welfare worker or care manager using a nationally standardized and computerized form. In addition, the applicant must receive a health assessment by his or her own physician. Using this information, a committee consisting of medical, social service, and local government personnel determine eligibility and level of care for which the person is qualified. The care level determines the yen-value of services which the person may receive, but which services will be actually used and which person or organization will provide them are decided by the elderly person, family members, and if desired, a care manager. The great majority of those who use services rely on a professional manager who arranges schedules of home nurses, home helpers, day care, equipment rentals, and applications for admission to nursing homes for short stays (respite care) or long-term residence.

Although everyone in our study was eligible for services, we found a great deal of variation in the extent to which these were actually used. In our sample of co-residing elderly, no one relied fully on professional services. Some decisions to not use services fully were based on personal preference, for example, one man who just did not like day care. The proportion of elderly who did not make use of any services was higher in Akita than in Tokyo, which may be related to the greater availability of family caregivers. However, there may also be differences in values. Rural-urban differences in lifestyle in the 1920s and 1930s, when today's eighty- and ninety-year-olds were growing up, were greater than they are today. However, before we conclude that the Akita people are more old-fashioned than the cosmopolitan Tokyoites, I should point out that our interviews as well as government surveys show that some people apply for long-term care insurance not with the intention of using services immediately, but rather to be eligible to be on a waiting list for institutional care. Although Akita has more nursing home beds per elderly population than Tokyo, the difficulties presented by the harsher climate and the lack of public transportation for shopping or medical appointments may make it more intimidating to try to manage at home.[5]

Some people calculate that it is best to get on board even if they are still managing relatively well, so that they do not have to become a burden on the family when they need more help. In the meantime, family support is sufficient and available.

Institutionalization of an elderly person for care may challenge traditional notions of *who* should be providing care for an ill or frail old person, but it does not challenge the cultural understanding that caregiving is one person's responsibility. The institution merely becomes a substitute for the daughter-in-law. This helps to explain the low rate of involvement of families in the lives of institutionalized elderly relatives that is frequently and unhappily noted by many nursing home directors (cf. Wu 2004, 139–54). However, the simultaneous use of family and professional caregivers in the home setting and the simultaneous use of multiple services inside and outside of the home have the potential to significantly change the cultural meaning of caregiving. This also, of course, contributes to new interpretations of family and of specific statuses within the family.

Someone's Borrowed

With and without long-term care services, dealing with challenging demographics regarding elder care is leading to changes in roles and statuses within the family. The lines of gender, birth order, and residence by which care responsibilities have been (at least ideally) distributed have become increasingly blurred. People are being "borrowed" from previously noncaregiving positions to take over or to assist in elder care.

Nationally, there has been a shift away from reliance on the eldest daughter-in-law to be the sole caregiver. Table 7.1 presents data from a 2001 national survey on who was the primary caregiver of elderly people. Wives and daughters-in-law predominate, but together constitute only about 40 percent of caregivers. Men now make up more than 16 percent of those providing family elder care.

In our long-term care study, the 2003 survey found an even higher proportion of husbands, sons, and daughters than in the national data, but there were large differences between the Tokyo and Akita samples. Wives were the most common caregiver in both locales, but more men and more daughters were primary caregivers in Tokyo. Daughters-in-law remained a significant source of care for the elderly in Akita (table 7.2).

Our interview subsample was purposively chosen so that we could interview people in a variety of relationships to the elderly person. The following sections offer examples of family responses to the need of

Table 7.1 Primary Caregivers of Frail Elderly People in Japan

Co-residing		66.1%
Husband	8.2%	
Wife	16.5	
Son	7.6	
Daughter	11.2	
Daughter-in-law	19.9	
Other relative	2.7	
Non-co-residing		33.9
Relative	8.7	
Paid care provider	13.6	
Other	6.0	
Unknown	5.6	

Source: Ministry of Health, Labor and Welfare, http://www8.cao.go.jp/kourei/whitepaper/w-2007/zenbun/html/j123200.html

Table 7.2 Relationship of Family Caregiver to Care Recipient in Project Survey and in National Survey

	Tokyo (%)	Akita (%)	Total for study (%)	National data[a] (%)
Husband	17.6	8.2	14.2	9.1
Wife	26.7	29.5	27.7	20.8
Son	13.1	11.9	12.6	9.2
Daughter	24.2	14.9	20.8	19.0
Son-in-law	0.4	0.0	0.3	0.3
Daughter-in-law	14.3	29.5	19.8	27.7
Other male	1.0	1.0	1.0	[b]
Other female	2.8	5.0	3.6	[b]

Notes:

a. This column presents data from a 2000 national survey of who was the primary caregiver of elders who were eligible for long-term care insurance system services. From *Kaigo sābisu setai chōsa* (Kōsei Rōdōshō, 2000).

b. In this survey, "other" is not broken down by gender. The total for "other" was 6.1 percent.

one of their elderly members for care. They combine some "traditional" ideas about caregiving with demographic realities and new services. The situations are not intended to represent "typical" families, but rather to portray a range of family caregiving decisions other than care by the wife or eldest daughter-in-law.

A Husband Caregiver

Mrs. Nakagawa is now eighty years old and is incapacitated because of a stroke. She cannot use her right arm, cannot walk independently, and speaks in a soft, slurred voice. Her husband is the main caregiver. The eighty-six-year-old is healthy, but hard of hearing and drinks too much for his wife's taste. She reports that he does some housework, including the laundry ("because there's a washing machine") and takes care of their small pet dog. However, they do not communicate well. She attributes this in part to the fact that she cannot raise her voice and he cannot hear, but she also points to differences in their upbringing. She was raised in Tokyo; he in the countryside up north. Both were together for the first interview; they frequently contradicted each other and expressed some resentment. In addition to the husband's help with housework, Mrs. Nakagawa was the recipient of long-term care services: she attended a day care program three times/week at which she also got a bath. She had a home helper come every day for several hours for personal care, including assistance in getting ready to go to day care.

In their case, the husband never seems to have made a commitment to his caregiver role. He is there and does what needs to be done (at least sometimes, according to the wife, who experiences great insecurity when he goes out drinking and comes home drunk, as she is not capable of getting help if anything happens), but he is happy to have the assistance of the home helpers. There is no one else to be the primary caregiver. The couple has three children. The oldest lives in another part of Tokyo, but they have no contact with him. Mrs. Nakagawa said he does not return their phone calls. The second is a daughter who just returned to the area with a thirteen-year-old daughter after separating from her husband because of his violence against her. She suffers from depression and must work for a living. The granddaughter recently failed a high school entrance exam. In general the Nakagawas' daughter does not seem to be in a position to help her parents much. The youngest of their children is a son who lives upstairs. He is a company employee and is unmarried. He occasionally helps take care of the dog, but apparently not his mother. He travels as part of his job and does not come home every night, so they cannot count on his help.

Thus, Mr. Nakagawa became primary caregiver by default. His lack of commitment to the role means that long-term care system services Mrs. Nakagawa receives are crucial to her well-being.

A Son Caregiver

In contrast, we interviewed a woman whose son had modified his life in part to be able to care for his mother in her old age. Eighty-four-year-old Mrs. Sakamoto had experienced surgery three times in the five years before we met her, once for breast cancer, once for colon polyps, and most recently for a hip fracture caused by a fall at home. Mrs. Sakamoto had three children, two daughters and a son, with whom she has good relationships. Her husband died many years ago, so she had lived on her own in her current house for nineteen years. About eight years prior to the interview, the son proposed that they remodel her house and that he, his wife, and their children move in with her because she was getting old and might need help some day. He saw elder care as primarily his responsibility as the eldest son (*chōnan*), but the arrangement also allowed him and his wife to follow their own interests more than they had been able to do when their children were young. They closed the family business which he had inherited from his father, his wife was able to pursue her dream of working as a dance teacher, and he could commit himself to a career as a writer, working at home while keeping an eye on his mother. Since Mrs. Sakamoto was able to get around with a walker and do most things on her own, even though slowly, there was no need for home helper services since her son and daughter-in-law were taking care of the household. One or the other of her two daughters comes to be with her if the son and his wife need to go out, and they invite her to stay with them for short periods and to travel with their families. I asked the son if there were ever disagreements among the siblings regarding their mother's care. He responded that he and his wife always let them know what is going on and consult with them, but everyone recognizes that they (the son and wife) are central; there haven't been any disagreements.

Mrs. Sakamoto is going to day care twice a week where, she claimed, the major benefit was recognizing that other people were in much worse shape than she. The son said that his greatest concern is with her mental state, for she has lost interest in doing much of anything, even things that in the past had given her much pleasure. He tries to encourage her to do as much as she can on her own because his mother has always been an independent person. She seems motivated to not become worse, even if she does not believe she will get better. Yet she is reluctant to do too much for fear of causing more trouble for her children. For example, she said she does not clear dishes from the table because she can't carry them well with the walker and if she drops them she will have created more of a mess than if she just let someone else clear. These ambivalent pulls toward independence and dependence seem to be the greatest problem for this family in caring for Mrs. Sakamoto. Although at one level, the son's caregiving is motivated by "traditional" filial piety, his decision allows him to pursue a nonconventional career. And of course he is a "borrowed" caregiver. Rather than turn the caregiving over to his wife, this eldest son has decided to take on the caregiver role himself.

A Daughter Caregiver

One of the daughter caregivers we met was successor in a large rural household. Mrs. Arai, the fifth of six children, had herself come with her husband to establish a branch household (*bunke*) on a piece of her father's land many years before. She is now ninety-three years old and has slight paralysis on her left side from a stroke in addition to heart and gastrointestinal disease. She and her husband had six children, four girls and then two boys, over a period of seventeen years. Thus, when her husband died in his fifties and she was not well enough to do the farming herself, the family struggled to keep the children in school long enough to graduate from middle school. The oldest daughter stayed to help her mother and younger siblings after she finished school. "There was no helping it (*Shikata nai*)," Mrs. Arai explained.

That her daughter was already living in her parents' home, that she is the successor, and that she is female made it "natural" that she be the caregiver when Mrs. Arai became older. But rather than see her role as caregiver for her elderly mother as a mere extension of her traditional roles, Mrs. Arai's daughter was proactive. Eight years before our first interview and thus six years before her mother's stroke, she began taking caregiving classes offered at the local nursing home, "because I thought I might need the knowledge in the future." One of the things she learned in her class was "Use your eyes but not your hands" (*Me o kakeru ga te o kakenai*). Thus, she tries to let her mother remain as independent as possible, a "modern" style of caregiving, similar to Mrs. Sakamoto's son's approach in the previous example.

When asked how the caregiver-care recipient relationship was going, Mrs. Arai responded, "I am grateful in my heart, but I don't say it."

A Younger Daughter-in-Law Caregiver

Mrs. Kajiyama was ninety-one years old when we interviewed her in 2003. She was quite demented, but she was able to continue to live at home due to the excellent care provided by her daughter-in-law and support from her son. However, this was not the eldest son, but rather her third son and his wife. There were eight children in the Kajiyama family, and the co-residing son was the fifth. It seems that there was a time when Mrs. Kajiyama lived with the eldest son and his wife, but it was before the third daughter-in-law married into the family. They have been living with Mrs. Kajiyama since their marriage. Mrs. Kajiyama farmed the land and the daughter-in-law worked for wages and took care of all the housework and cooking. Mrs. Kajiyama's husband had apparently deserted the family. After his death, the eldest son had kept his father's memorial tablet until his own death ten years ago. The second son married into a local family as an adopted heir (*yōshi*). He does not participate in Mrs. Kajiyama's regular care, but visits occasionally, and he took his mother in to stay at his home for four months after there was a major fire in the third son's home two years before the interview. The four daughters call or visit more rarely, and are not involved in caregiving or care decisions.

Thus, for Mrs. Kajiyama, the caregiving by the third daughter-in-law is a substitution for the wife of the eldest son, a "natural" extension of the daughter-in-law's gender-based role in the household. Yet unlike the stereotypical mother-in-law—daughter-in-law relationship, the situation seemed to have surprisingly little tension. Mrs. Kajiyama's daughter-in-law explained that there had been a lot more strain in their relationship in the past. Even then, however, they didn't argue much because there was no time for arguing. Mrs. Kajiyama worked in the fields from morning to evening. When the daughter-in-law came home from work, she had housework and cooking and care for her own two daughters. The retirement of her husband several years ago provided some relief and the daughters are now grown and living away. After the fire at their home, the daughter-in-law did not return to her paid job. So she has more time and less stress, and says it is easier to be kind now. Moreover, now that her mother-in-law has become more demented, she is milder and easier to have around. Mrs. Kajiyama also goes to day care two days a week and occasionally for respite care to a local nursing home. That allows the son and daughter-in-law a little time, for the first time in their adult lives, to pursue their own interests. But the daughter-in-law often uses that time to care for her own eighty-three-year-old mother, who lives in a nearby town. She is the only one of her siblings who lives in the area.

A More Old-Fashioned Kind of Daughter-in-Law Caregiver

Globalization has introduced another category of "borrowed" caregiver, that of foreign daughters-in-law (*gaijin yome*). In my interviews in the last several years, I have heard of two examples of this direct link between the globalized experiences of some Japanese and who is available for family caregiving of the elderly. One case was the marriage of a son of a good friend of a woman I was interviewing. She mentioned that her friend has talked about the daughter-in-law in terms of a potential need for elder care. The other case was a different respondent's own son; the issue of elder care was not directly salient for her since when I met her she was in a hospice with terminal cancer.

In both cases, these were East Asian brides, one from China and one from Korea. They were not poor farmers' daughters coming to marry the brideless men of rural Akita, although as in other areas of rural Japan, finding Japanese women willing to move on to a husband's family farm can be a challenge. Rather, these were foreign women whom educated, upper-middle-class men met when they were abroad for their jobs or education. The friend of the woman who had a Korean daughter-in-law reported that the friend was a little worried about cultural differences between the couple, but liked the young woman. The friend had also commented that the Koreans were more filial than the Japanese and so thought the daughter-in-law would care for her and her husband when they were old. The woman in the hospice had similar thoughts about her Chinese daughter-in-law. She did not seem too pleased with the international marriage (*kokusai kekkon*). She complained to me that the daughter-in-law's Japanese intonation is terrible and that she herself admits it. But, she continued, she is a stricter parent than my other daughter-in-law, "in some sense, more Japanese." When I asked about mother-in-law—daughter-in-law relations in China, she said she did not know but, "In China, they take good care of their parents, don't they?"(*Chūgoku dewa oya o daiji ni suru deshō*). She concluded this part of our conversation by saying, "She seems like a good person."

Shared Caregiving

The final example of new categories of people doing the caregiving is that of the sharing of responsibility among family members. Because caregiving has historically been allocated to a single person, this is a departure from the model of traditional family roles. To work well, it requires good communication and trust across sibling relationships.

One situation which seemed to be working quite well was that of Mrs. Nishimura, now eighty-one years old. She suffers from Parkinson's disease and at the time of the second interview was in a rehabilitation hospital recovering from surgery after breaking her hip. Mrs. Nishimura had married a salaryman in Niigata before the war, but her husband went into the military and died of a war injury not long after returning home, leaving Mrs. Nishimura to work as a nurse and raise their two daughters on her own. Both daughters' marriages took them to other parts of the country, so Mrs. Nishimura lived alone for thirty years. About a year before our first interview with her, Mrs. Nishimura had moved in with her second daughter and twenty-nine-year-old granddaughter in their small condominium in Tokyo, which they remodeled to be "barrier-free" with the assistance of long-term care insurance funds.

Both of Mrs. Nishimura's two daughters were present when we asked how she came to Tokyo rather than to the older daughter's home in the Kansai region. Both daughters are also widowed and all of their children are old enough to no longer need much parental attention. Both had good relations with their mother. They noted that their mother had spent time as a child with her grandfather in Tokyo, so the city was more familiar, making it an easier move. Yet the condo was in a totally different part of town; it was very quiet and had a suburban feel. The sisters agreed that the mother had a preference for Tokyo, but they also suggested that it came down to personality. The older sister explained that she had the type of personality that would worry about each little thing and she would get very stressed at her mother's decline. Her sister added, "Because she's too caring. For me, I am more laid back, and just figure these changes happen as people get older."

The younger daughter was thus the primary caregiver, but at the time of the first interview was working about thirty hours/week. The granddaughter, a nurse like her grandmother had been, helped out, especially with medical questions. Mrs. Nishiyama went to day care twice a week, and a home helper came five times/week for a total of six hours. On the day care days, they helped Mrs. Nishiyama get ready to go out so that her daughter could get to work. On other days, they assisted with personal care and sometimes took her for walks in her wheelchair. But in addition to these long-term care services, the younger sister received help from the older sister, who came one week each month to take a turn as primary caregiver. In the spring, Mrs. Nishiyama and the second daughter had gone back to the family home in Niigata to visit with Mrs. Nishiyama's old friends. There, she fell and fractured her hip. Her second daughter was there when it happened, but soon, the older daughter came up from Kansai to watch her mother (who was in the hospital) so that the younger daughter could go back to work. The older daughter stayed for a month until Mrs. Nishiyama was discharged, and brought her to Tokyo. Once Mrs. Nishiyama was settled in the rehabilitation hospital, the older daughter returned to her own home.

Why was their situation so different from the usual single-caregiver model? One factor may be that caregiving responsibilities are often linked explicitly or implicitly to inheritance, but in this case there did not seem to be much of an inheritance to worry about except for the house in Niigata. Secondly, there were no sons in the family. The daughters had not grown up with their father around, and perhaps there was no expectation of household continuity in such a household. Scott Clark (1999) has suggested that relationships among sisters may be especially close and meaningful despite the lack of attention to these relationships in most discussions of Japanese family dynamics. Furthermore, that all three women were widowed (one of them referred to themselves as a "trio of widows") and the granddaughter being still single meant that there were few other obligations that would compete with their desire to take care of Mrs. Nishiyama. But it seems to me that the major factor was their desire to do it, based on their obvious love and respect for their mother both as a person and for her earlier sacrifices on their behalf. Finally, Mrs. Nishiyama is appreciative, and frequently expresses how difficult it is to be dependent and how grateful she is for their care.

Someone's Blue

The story of the daughters is a happy resolution to that family's twin problems of no sons and no child remaining in the family home. Mrs. Nishi-yama, both daughters, and the co-residing granddaughter all seem pleased with the current arrangements. Although they acknowledge that caregiver strain and normal mother-daughter arguments are part of the picture, the family has successfully passed through a new health crisis this past year, and they vow to continue to take good care of Mrs. Nishiyama.

But "borrowing" caregivers to resolve the problem of who will take care of an elderly family member does not necessarily assure that things go well. Some people who take on that role are ill-prepared by training and experience, or by personality, to meet the standards of being a good caregiver. The gap between age- and gender-based role expectations and the reality of their daily lives is difficult, especially for some of the men. Moreover, since care from these sources cannot be assumed, it must be negotiated and thus must become explicit. In many families, open patterns of communication are difficult, and the role of the elderly person in the decision-making process is not always clear, or agreed upon among major players.

For example, Mr. Nakagawa, the husband described earlier, was an eighty-six-year-old raised in the countryside in a huge family before the war. He had no domestic skills when he took over running the house-hold after his wife's stroke. Moreover, his continued habit of going out drinking caused his wife tremendous insecurity. Mrs. Nakagawa told us of one night when he came home so drunk he fell in the entryway and hit his head. She then had the additional problem of getting to the phone and calling her daughter in the middle of the night so that they could get an ambulance to the house to take him to the hospital. (Due to her stroke, Mrs. Nakagawa would have had a difficult time making herself heard and understood if she had tried to make the call directly.) Mrs. Nakagawa herself went to a nursing home for a "short stay" (respite care) while he was hospitalized. In another similar situation of a husband caregiver, the husband was very charming when we spoke with him, presenting himself as an organized home manager, but, in a separate interview, the wife claimed that his neglect of her care and verbal tirades amounted to abuse.

A second type of difficulty lies in the gap between expectations and reality regarding gender roles. After all, women are supposed to be the ones who do housework, care for the sick, and nurture the family. A man who had been the main caregiver of his parents some years before in Osaka talked about his relationships at work. He recalled that in the late 1980s, before there were many services available to help family care-givers, his mother had been hospitalized with heart and lung problems. His father had dementia and was extremely difficult because of both his personality and his illness. He was the only son of five siblings and thus felt an obligation to care for his parents. His wife worked full time, and in any case it did not seem that she was inclined to try to handle her demented father-in-law. They hired an older woman housekeeper to be with his father during the day so the son could go to work, but whenever the slightest thing happened, he was called to come handle it. "They put up with it at work," he recalled, "but it really caused problems for my co-workers." He believed that because he had to leave earlier than his colleagues and was unable to fully participate at work, he lost out on any chances for promotion. He seemed to have coped with this loss of status in the workplace by becoming involved after his parents died in a family support group where he was an officer at the time of our interview with him in the mid-1990s.

In another family, a husband caregiver in his sixties with a wife bedridden with rheumatoid arthritis, had returned to the family after a career in the military. The husband and wife had little to say to each other. They had little contact with their daughter; an unmarried son lived with them but provided little assistance in caring for his mother. The husband said his wife always complained about the manner in which he cared for her and told the interviewer that if only there was a daughter-in-law, he would not have to do this. He was both resigned and resentful.

An additional source of caregiving blues is communication problems within families. We interviewed a retired man in 2004 who had been car-ing, with his working wife's help, for his mother. Unlike the men who had difficulty crossing the old gender boundaries, this retired salaryman enjoyed it. He cooked lunch for his wife (she worked nearby so came home for lunch) and after his mother was put into a rehabilitation facility several months earlier, visited her frequently. In addition, he has taken a job as a nurse's aide in a nearby dialysis center three days a week. Yet there has been a major fallout with his sister who also lives in Tokyo such that she had not even been informed about the worsening of her mother's condition. The son said they have had no contact for a couple of years. The mother seemed sad through her dementia when she told us, "She doesn't know that I am here [in the nursing home]."

Sometimes, there is communication, but of the negative variety. In one family where the daughter-in-law was the primary caregiver, the older woman's own daughter lived next door. The daughter-in-law told us that the daughter prepares breakfast for her mother and does her laundry. My first reaction was, "Oh, how wonderful that she is willing to share the burden." It was a good thing I didn't say what I was thinking, because the daughter-in-law proceeded to tell us that this "help" was done in the spirit of criticism. The daughter-in-law made western-style breakfasts because that was what her husband preferred, but her mother-in-law wanted Japanese-style meals. The daughter did her mother's laundry because the daughter-in-law didn't do it properly. When we had a second interview a year later, one of the first things the daughter-in-law told us was that her sister-in-law had been forced by her own family's circumstances to move to the northern island of Hokkaidō. The daughter-in-law's main concern seemed to be that she stay there!

Not to be omitted from the blues is the general sadness of becoming old, frail, and dependent for the old people themselves. This was best expressed by someone with perhaps the most ideal caregiving situation, Mrs. Sakamoto. Mrs. Sakamoto was not complaining about her son and daughter-in-law, but rather was making observations about life in the twenty-first century from the perspective of someone born in the Taisho period (1912–1926):

> Young people don't cook from scratch, and they don't make the flavors I'm used to from the old days.... We used to take the kids on a family vacation every summer. Now *they* take *me*.... I used to play the *shamisen*,[6] but now with my lower back pain I can't sit on the floor any more, but I can't live my life in chairs either.... I wish they had more television programs of interest to old people.... I have a lot of friends in the neighborhood, but they're all dying or can't go out any more.... Seeing the

other people at day care makes me realize there are a lot of people worse than I. . . . It makes me worry about what will happen in the future. . . .

When we were leaving and asked if we could come back to talk with them next year, Mrs. Sakamoto replied, "If I'm still here." She said this with a smile, and she clearly appreciates her family's care. Yet like so many of the older people with whom we spoke, there is nothing much positive to be said for getting old, ill, frail, and dependent.

Conclusion

I have attempted to show through examples from interviews that Japanese families cope with demographic realities of the need for elder care as they have dealt with inheritance and succession in the past: with pragmatism, with the blurring of gender and birth order roles, and with the localization of new ideas, values, and even categories of people in the case of the foreign daughters-in-law. Although not equal in status and power, as in all areas of life, culture offers multiple models of elder care. For contemporary Japanese, the versions of who should be the caregiver include not only early twentieth century ideals of eldest daughter-in-law, but also "modern" notions of daughters and husbands and professionals providing care for the elderly. In real life, choices must be made in line with circumstances as least as much as with ideals. Culture provides options and meanings, but does not determine behavior. As P. Bourdieu (1977) emphasizes in his concept of habitus, human agency must remain central to any understanding of behavior. Japanese families do not automatically respond to the need for elder care with the "traditional" approach, not do they obediently follow the latest international trends reported in the media as "modern." Rather, they examine the situation in front of them, consider the options, and pick and chose from among them to resolve the situation, although all choices will not be perceived as equally good ones by others.

This is because culture also shapes, but does not determine, the way people respond to the variations of caregiving that families adopt. Achieving cultural ideals may be impossible for some, creating personal disappointments and tensions in interpersonal relationships. We often in our interviews heard expressions of resentment, stress, anger, and extreme sadness. With a schedule of care activities that varies by day of the week and hour of the day, it must feel to some older people, raised with assumptions of caregiving as a solo role, as though *no* one is in charge. Others would prefer that the "proper" person take on the role of caregiver. Uncertainty about the future and uncertainty over their caregiver's commitment to the job adds insecurity to the other negative emotions some of the older people feel. Caregivers feel unfairly criticized, overwhelmed, and a sense of loss of what their lives might have been at work or at home.

Yet this is not to say that everyone is always miserable. Caregivers we have interviewed have expressed some satisfaction in doing what one can, especially for a parent or a spouse who has provided nurturance in the past. Some express pride in the new skills acquired to become caregivers. Some elderly people have commented that they are more comfortable with a daughter than a daughter-in-law, or note with satisfaction that in utilizing external service providers, they are not such a burden on their children. Everyone we spoke with welcomed the greater availability of services, even if they chose not to use them or thought the system too expensive or bureaucratic. Even those who had criticisms of the system were generally appreciative of the care providers whose services they used.

It is too soon to draw conclusions about how these new experiences of "something new" and "someone borrowed" will change the Japanese family. The long-term care insurance system was established in response to demographic and family changes. Those who debated what kind of policy should be created also recognized that the resulting system would have the potential to alter families as well. Perhaps the availability of in-home services will make it less likely that frail elderly will need to live with their children; on the other hand, day care and respite care may make the job of caregiver less onerous for wives and daughters-in-law. We can predict that new services and borrowed caregivers will allow greater experimentation with combinations of styles and expand the range of options for Japanese caregiving, altering expectations for future generations. More options also mean the need for better communication among members of the family on issues of care and family relationships. This type of social change comes not directly from policy or from the introduction of new ideas, but rather from the accumulated experiences of many individuals with new, sometimes less than ideal, situations.

In the short run, there is a great deal of sadness and sense of loss for both the elderly and their caregivers. In the long run, changes in family configuration, caregiving roles, and the meaning of family may realign into an easier fit. Yet there will likely remain strains between the reality of people's lives and the cultural ideals they or others think they should achieve. The elder care issue which now receives such attention is for anthropologists of Japan another reminder of the application of human ingenuity to try to bridge that gap.

Notes

Someone's Old, Something's New, Someone's Borrowed, Someone's Blue

The data for this chapter come primarily from an interdisciplinary project on elder care entitled, "Care for the Elderly Since the Enactment of Public Long Term Care Insurance in Japan: A Qualitative Study," funded by grants from the Japanese Ministries of Education and Science and of Health, Labor, and Welfare and led by Suda Yūko and Takahashi Ryūtarō. The chapter also draws upon interviews from a 1996 ethnographic research project in the Hanshin area that focused on end-of-life decisions, funded by an Abe Fellowship. The author would like to express her deepest appreciation to those families and individuals who participated in the interviews. Special thanks are also due to co-interviewers in 1996, Phyllis Braudy Harris and Fujii Miwa, and in the 2003 and 2004 long-term care project, Asakawa Noriko, Asano Yūko, Ruth Campbell, Kodama Hiroko, Izumo Yūji, Muraoka Kōko, Nishimura Chie, Nishida Masumi, Takahashi Ryūtarō, and Yamada Yoshiko. Keith Brown, Takahashi Ryūtarō, and John Traphagan offered helpful suggestions on an earlier draft of this chapter.

1. See Robert J. Smith's presidential address to the Association for Asian Studies, entitled, "Something Old, Something New" (Smith 1989).

2. The project is part of a five-year longitudinal study with both quantitative and qualitative components. The first stage was a large-scale survey in 2003 of family caregivers and care recipients, approximately fifteen hundred people in a largely working-class ward of Tokyo and in a small city and surrounding area in Akita. Several months after the survey, we conducted follow-up semistructured interviews of thirty care recipient-family caregiver pairs after obtaining their informed consent. Respondents were visited in their homes by two or three researchers. They were selected to include both men and women as care recipients, and a range of (insurance system) care levels and relationships to the primary family caregiver. Additional rounds of interviews were conducted with these respondents yearly through 2007.

In both locations, the majority of care recipients were female. Their age ranged from sixty-five to ninety-three years old, with an average age of eighty-one years. Their problems ranged from light to severe. All of the elderly in this sample, by design, were qualified for at least a minimal level of assistance for the long-term care insurance system and were co-residing in some fashion or another with a family caregiver. Thus, the caregivers described in this chapter do not include those who are resisting taking on the care of elderly relatives as described by J. Traphagan (2003).

3. Of households containing people sixty-five and older in 2005, 37.5 percent included co-residence with a child; 29.2 percent were older couple only households; and 22.0 percent lived alone. Only 45 years earlier, 86 percent were living with an adult child.

4. In 2003, women made up 41 percent of the Japanese labor force. In 1984, 57 percent of Japanese women participated in paid work; by 2003 that figure was up to 64 percent (Ministry of Internal Affairs and Communications 2005).

5. Izumo Yūji, personal communication, October 22, 2004. Statistics on the availability of nursing home beds of various types per population of those sixty-five and older by prefecture can be found at the Ministry of Health, Labor and Welfare web site http://www.mhlw.go.jp/toukei/saikin/hw/kaigo/service02/kekka3.html.

6. The *shamisen* is a three-stringed musical instrument of the lute family. It is played sitting on the floor with knees bent and feet tucked under, a position that Mrs. Sakamoto could not assume because of the hip fracture.

References

AERA. 2005. *Neo-kekkon no katachi.* [The forms of neo-marriage]. 18:16–19.

Allison, A. 2000. *Permitted and Prohibited Desires: Mothers, Comics, and Censorship in Japan.* Berkeley, CA: University of California Press.

Anpo o Tatakau Fujin Renrakukai, ed. 1969. *Kyūen nōto.* Tokyo, Kyūen Renraku Sentā.

Aoki, T. 1990. *Nihon bunkaron no henyō: Sengo nihon no bunka to aidentitī* [The Changing Treatise on 'Japanese Culture': Postwar Japanese Culture and Identity]. Tokyo: Chūōkōronsha.

Arai, M. 1986. *Koneko chibinke to chishibari no hana: Miketsushu jūichi nen no seishun* [Kitty Chibinke and Chishibari Flowers: A Youth of Eleven Years in Unconvicted Detention]. Tokyo, Komichi Shobō.

Asahi Shinbun Tēma Danwashitsu. 1988. *Kazoku: Nihonjin no kazokukan.* Tokyo: Asahi Sonorama.

Bernstein, G. L. 1991. "Introduction." In *Recreating Japanese Women, 1600–1945.* Edited by Gail Lee Bernstein, 1–14. Berkeley, CA: University of California Press.

Bourdieu, P. 1977. *Outline of a Theory of Practice.* Translated by Richard Nice. Cambridge: Cambridge University Press.

Brown, L. K. 1966. "Dōzoku and the Ideology of Descent in Rural Japan." *American Anthropologist,* 68:1129–1151.

Cabinet Office. 2003. Annual report on the aging society. Web site: http:// www8.cao.go.jp/kourei/english/annualreport/2003/fl-2-05.html

Campbell, J. C. 2000. "Changing Meanings of Frail Old People and the Japanese Welfare State." In *Caring for the Elderly in Japan and the US: Practices and Policies.* Edited by S. O. Long, 82–97. London: Routledge.

Castberg, A. D. 1990. *Japanese Criminal Justice.* New York, Praeger Publishers.

Castells, M. 1997. *The Power of Identity.* Oxford: Blackwell.

Cohen, D., and Eisdofer, C. (1986). *The Loss of Self: A Family Resource for the Care of Alzheimer's Disease and Related Disorders.* New York: Norton.

Clark, S. 1999. "My Other House: Lifelong Relationships among Sisters of the Hayashi Family." In *Lives in Motion: Composing Circles of Self and Community in Japan.* Edited by S. O. Long, 41–58. Ithaca: Cornell University East Asia Program.

Daidō, T., and H. Suzuki. 1988. *Nitchū no hazama ni ikite: jibun de kaita zanryū koji no kiroku* [Having Lived in between Japan and China: Records Genuinely Written by Zanryū Koji]. Tokyo: Shin Jidaisha.

della Porta, D. 1995. *Social Movements, Political Violence, and The State: A Comparative Analysis of Italy and Germany.* New York, Cambridge University Press.

Dower, J. 1999. *Embracing Defeat: Japan in the Wake of World War II.* New York: W. W. Norton.

Duus, P. 1988. "Introduction." In *Japan Inc.: An Introduction to Japanese Economics* (the Comic Book). Edited by S. Ishimori. Berkeley, CA: University of California Press.

Flacks, R., and J. Whalen 1989. *Beyond the Barricades.* Philadelphia, Temple University Press.

Gauntlett, D. 2003. "Preface." In *Japanese Cybercultures.* Edited by N. Gottlieb and M. McLelland, xii–xv. New York: Routledge.

Giddens, A. 1992. *The Transformation of Intimacy: Sexuality, Love, and Eroticism in Modern Societies.* Stanford, CA: Stanford University Press.

———. 2000. *Runaway World: How Globalization is Reshaping Our Lives.* New York: Routledge.

Goessmann, H. M. 2000. "New Role Models for Men and Women? Gender in Japanese TV Dramas." In Japan Pop! : *Inside the World of Japanese Popular Culture.* Edited by T. J. Craig, 207–21. Armonk, NY: M. E. Sharpe, 2000.

Goodman, R., ed. 2002. *Family and Social Policy in Japan: Anthropological Approaches, Contemporary Japanese Society.* Cambridge, UK: Cambridge University Press, 2002

Gross, J. 2004. "Alzheimer's in the Living Room: How One Family Rallies to Cope." *New York Times,* September 14, p. A 1, p. A 22.

Haneda, S. 2000. *Eiga to watakushi* [Film and I]. Tokyo: Shōbunsha.

———. 2006, October 26. *Owari yokereba subete yoshi* [All Will be All Right If the Last Moment Is Well Taken Care Of], Program note, 1.

Hareven, T. K. 1978. *Transitions: The Family and the Life Course in Historical Perspective,* New York: Academic Press.

Harootunian, H. D. 1989. "Visible Discourses/Invisible Ideologies." In *Postmodernism and Japan.* Edited by M. Miyoshi and H. D. Harootunian, 63–92. Durham, NC: Duke University Press.

Hasegawa, M. 1997. *The Wonderful World of Sazae-san.* Vol. 1. Translated by Jules Young. Bilingual Comics. Tokyo: Kodansha International.

Hasegawa, M. 2001. *Granny Mischief* [Ijiwaru Bāsan]. Translated by Jules Young. Bilingual Comics. Tokyo: Kodansha International.

Hashimoto, A. 1996. *The Gift of Generations: Japanese and American Perspectives on Aging and the Social Contact.* New York: Cambridge University Press.

———. 1997. "Designing Family Values: Cultural Assumptions of an Aging Society." *Japan Quarterly* 44, No. 4: 59–65.

———. 2000. "Cultural Meaning of 'Security' in Aging Policies." In *Caring for the elderly in Japan and the U.S.: Practices and Policies.* Edited by Susan Orpett Long, 19–27. London: Routledge.

————. 2004a. "Culture, Power and the Discourse of Filial Piety in Japan: The Disempowerment of Youth and Its Social Consequences." In *Filial Piety: Practice and Discourse in Contemporary East Asia*. Edited by C. Ikels, 182–97. Stanford, CA: Stanford University Press.

————. 2004b. "Power to the Imagination." Woodrow Wilson International Center for Scholars Asia Program *Special Report* 121:9–12.

Hashimoto, A., and C. Ikels. 2005. "Filial Piety in Changing Asian Societies." In *Cambridge Handbook on Age and Ageing*. Edited by Malcolm Johnson, 437–42. Cambridge: Cambridge University Press.

Hashimoto, A., and J. W. Traphagan. "Manga ni miru Nihon no kazoku" [Family Relations in Japanese Manga]. *Gendai no Esupuri* [L'esprit D'aujourd'hui] 444:213–19.

Hayashi, I. 1986. *Manshū: sono maboroshi no kuni yueni* [Manchuria: A Country of Illusion]. Tokyo: Chikuma Shobō.

Held, D., A. McGrew, D. Goldblatt, and J. Perraton. 1999. *Global Transformations: Politics, Economics and Culture*. Stanford, CA: Stanford University Press.

Higuchi, K. 2002. " 'Mukashiwa yokatta' no omoikomi" [The Belief in the Good Old Days]. *Bungei shunjū* April *special issue*, 147–48.

————. 2006. *"Sazae-san: Ninki no himitsu"* [Sazae-san: Secrets of Her Popularity. In Sazae-San No 'Shōwa' [Sazae-san's 'Shōwa']. Edited by S. Tsurumi and S. Saitō, 116–50. Tokyo: Kashiwa Shobō.

Himori, C. 2005. "Totsuide kara no ayumi (bassui)" [Steps After My Marriage (excerpt)]. In *Suiheisen no mukō ni: Ruporutāju Himori Kōyū* [Beyond the Horizon: Reportage of Himori Kōyū]. Edited by Suiheisen no Mukō ni Henshū Iinkai, 21–24. Tokyo, Fūjinsha.

Himori, K. 1999. *Nihon sekigun sokuseiki o meguru oboegaki* [Memorandum Concerning the Founding of the Japanese Red Army]. Han [Revolt].

Holden, Todd and Takako Tsuruki. 2003. "Deaikai: Japan's New Culture of Encounter." In *Japanese Cybercultures*. Edited by N. Gottlieb and M. McLelland, 34–49. New York: Routledge.

Ishii, H. 2002a. *Nono-chan*. Tokyo: Futabasha.

————. 2002b. *Tonari no Yamada-kun* [My Neighbors Yamada] 1. Tokyo: Sōgensha.

Ishiko, J. 1989. *Sengo manga no shujinkōtachi* [The Protagonists of Postwar Japanese Manga]. Tokyo: Kusanone Shuppankai.

Ivy, M. 1995. *Discourses of the Vanishing: Modernity, Phantasm, Japan*. Chicago: University of Chicago Press.

Iwamoto, S. 1997. "Blondie (1): Americanization in Japan after the Second World War." *Kansai gakuin daigaku shakaigakubu kiyō* 78:155–67.

————. 1998. "Blondie (2): Americanization in Japan after the Second World War." *Kansai gakuin daigaku shakaigakubu kiyō* 79:147–60.

Japan Center for Intercultural Communication. 2005. International Comparison: Ratio of 65 Year Old and Over among Total Population (1990–2050). Japan Information Network. Web site: http://web-jpn.org//stat/stats/01CEN2C.html.

Jenike, B. R. 2003. "Parent Care and Shifting Family Obligations in Urban Japan." In *Demographic Change and the Family in Japan's Aging Society*. Edited by J. W. Traphagan and J. Knight, 177–202. Albany: State University of New York Press.

Jin'no, M. 1992. *"Manshū" ni okurareta on'na-tachi: tairiku no hanayome* [The Women Who Were Sent to Manchuria: The Continental Brides]. Kyoto: Nashinoki sha.

Johnson, D. T. 2002. *The Japanese Way of Justice: Prosecuting Crime in Japan.* New York: Oxford University Press.

Kamitsubo, T. 1979. Mizuko no fu: hikiage koji to okasareta on'na-tachi no Kiroku [The Epitaph for the Aborted Fetuses: The Records of Repatriated Orphans and Rape Victims]. Tokyo: Tokuma Shoten.

Kataoka, Y. 1985. *Bakudan sedai no shōgen* [Testimony from the Bomb Generation]. Tokyo: San'ichi Shobō.

Kawashima, T. 1950. *Nihon shakai no kazokuteki kōsei* [The Family Structure of Japanese Society]. Tokyo: Nihon Hyōronsha.

Kinsella, A. 2000. *Adult Manga: Culture and Power in Contemporary Japanese Society.* Honolulu: University of Hawai'i Press.

Konigsberg, I. (1987). *The Complete Film Dictionary.* New York: New American Library.

Kōsei-shō (The Japanese Ministry of Health and Welfare). 1947/48. *Hikiage ken'eki-shi* [The History of the Quarantine for the Repatriates]. 3 Vols. Tokyo: Hikiage Ken'eki-kyoku.

———. 1978. *Hikiage to engo sanjū-nen no ayumi* [The Repatriation and the Assistance Extended to the Repatriates]. Tokyo: Gyōsei.

———. 1997. *Engo gojū-nen-shi* [The 50 Years of History of the Assistance Extended to the Repatriates]. Tokyo: Gyōsei.

Kotani, M. 1997. *Seibo Ebuangerion.* Tokyo: Magazine House.

Kriesi, H., R. Koopmans, et al. 1992. "New Social Movements and Political Opportunities in Western Europe." *European Journal of Political Research* 22:219–44.

Kyūen Renraku Sentā, ed. 1973. *Anata ni nobiru Nachisu no te o tatte* [Cut Off the Nazi Hand That is Coming Toward You]. Tokyo: Kyūen Renraku Sentā.

———, ed. 1977. *Kyūen nōto.* Tokyo: Kyūen Renraku Sentā.

———, ed. 1978. *Kyūen nōto.* Tokyo: Kyūen Renraku Sentā.

Kyūen Shukusatsuban Kankō Iinkai, ed. 1977. *Kyūen Shukusatsuban* 1968/12– 1977/8, *sōkangō-100 gō* [Kyūen, Reduced Print Edition 12/1968–8/1977, First Issue–#100]. Tokyo: Kyūen Renraku Sentā.

Laslett, P. 1972. *Household and Family in Past Time.* Cambridge: Cambridge University Press.

Lee, W. 2000. "From Sazae-San to Crayon Shin-Chan: Family Amine, Social Change, and Nostalgia in Japan." In *Japan Pop! : Inside the World of Japanese Popular Culture.* Edited by Timothy J. Craig, 186–202. Armonk, NY: M. E. Sharpe.

Long, S. O. 1997. Risōteki na kaigo to wa? Amerika kara mita nihon no rinen to genjitsu [What is Ideal Caregiving? Japanese Ideals and Reality from an American's Perspective]. *Hosupisu to zaitaku kea* [Hospice Care and Home Care] 5, No. 1: 37–43.

———, ed. 2000. *Caring for the Elderly in Japan and the U.S: Practices and Policies.* London and New York: Routledge.

Mainichi Shinbun. 2004. "Atarashii kekkonkan: Dōsei erabu josei ga fueru." September 1, 2004. http://www.mainichi-msn.co.jp/column/shasetsu/index.html (accessed September 2, 2004).

Manshū Kaitaku-shi Kankō-kai, ed. 1984a. *Nagano-ken manshū kaitaku-shi: sōron* [The History of Colonization of Manchuria by the Agrarian Immigrants from Nagano Prefecture: Overview]. Nagano: Nagano-ken Kaitaku Jikōkai.

———, ed. 1984b. *Nagano-ken manshū kaitaku-shi: kaku-dan-hen* [The History of Colonization of Manchuria by the Agrarian Immigrants from Nagano Prefecture: Individual Agrarian Colonies]. Nagano: Nagano-ken Kaitaku Jikōkai.

Maruoka, O. 1990. *Kōan Keisatsu [Marukō] Nanbo no monja* [Who Are these Security Police Anyhow?]. Tokyo: Shinsensha.

Matsui, H. 2002. "Oriume o megutte: Taidan" [About Oriume: Round table discussion]. *Shinario* 58, No. 4: 18–32.

———. 1998. "Production Notes." *Cine Switch* 5, No. 4: 18–32.

Matsumoto, Y. 1996. *Eiga o tsukutta on'natachi: josei kantoku no hyakunen* [Women filmmakers: A one-hundred year history of women directors]. Tokyo: Cinema House.

McAdam, D., and R. Paulsen 1993. "Specifying the Relationship Between Social Ties and Activism." *American Journal of Sociology* 99: 640–67.

Meguro, Y. 1987. *Kojinka suru kazoku* [The Individualizing Family]. Tokyo: Keisō Shobō.

Ministry of Internal Affairs and Communications, Statistical Bureau. 2005. Population 15 Years Old and Older by Labor Force Status. Retrieved from Japan Statistical Yearbook. January 21, 2005. Web site: http://www.stat.go.jp/data/nenkan/pdf/y1601000.pdf.

Mitchell, R. H. 1992. *Janus-Faced Justice: Political Criminals in Imperial Japan.* Honolulu: University of Hawai'i Press.

Mitome, T. 1988. *Manshū kimin* [The Abandoned People in Manchuria]. Tokyo: Tokyo Shoseki.

Mitsuhashi, C. 1984. *Hāi Ak'ko desu* [Hi, I'm Ak'ko]. Tokyo: Tachikaze shobō.

Miura, A. 1999. *'Kazoku' to 'kōfuku' no sengoshi: Kōgai no yume to genjitsu.* Tokyo: Kōdansha.

Miyagawa, M. 1973. "Kindai izen no kazoku: Chūsei." In *Kōza kazoku: Kazoku no rtekishi.* Edited by Michio Aoyama, Takeda, Tōru Arichi, Itsuo Emori, and Haruo Matsubara, 46–75. Tokyo: Kōbundō.

Morioka, K. 1984. *Ie no henbō to senzo no matsuri* [Changes in the Household and Ancestral Rites]. Tokyo: Nihon Kirisutokyōdan Shuppan Kyoku.

Murakami, Y., S. Kumon, and S. Satō. 1979. *Bunmei to Shite No Ie Shakai* [Family Society as Civilization]. Tokyo: Chūōkōronsha.

164   *References*

Muta, K. 1996. *Senryaku to shiteno kazoku: Kindai nihon no kokumin kokka keisei to josei.* Tokyo: Shinyōsha.
Naikakufu (Cabinet Office). 2003. Heisei 16 nenpan kōrei shakai hakusho (White Paper on the Aging Society, 2003). Web site: http://www8.cao.go.jp/kourei/whitepaper/w-2004/zenbun/16index.html.
Nakane, C. 1967. *Tateshakai no ningen kankei* [Social Relations in A Vertical Society]. Tokyo: Kōdansha.
Nakanishi, S. 2004. *Wakamonotachi ni naniga okotteirunoka* [What's happening to the Youths?]. Tokyo: Kadensha.
Napier, S. 1996. *The Subversion of Modernity: The Fantastic in Modern Japanese Literature: The Subversion of Modernity.* London: Routledge.
———. 2002. "When the Machines Stop: Terminal Identities in Modern Japanese Animation." *Science Fiction Studies* 29, No. 3: 418–35.
———. 2005. "The Problem of Existence in Japanese Animation." *Bulletin of the American Philosophical Society.*
Nihon Seishōnen Kenkyūjo. 2004. *Kōkōsei no gakushū ishiki to nichijō seikatsu: Nihon, amerika, chūgoku no 3 kakoku hikaku.* Tokyo: Nihon Seishōnen Kenkyūjo.
Nonini, D., and A. Ong. 1997. "Chinese Transnationalism as an Alternative Modernity." In *Ungrounded Empires: The Cultural Politics of Modern Chinese Transnationalism.* Edited by A. Ong and D. Nonini, 3–33. New York: Routledge.
Nōson Kōsei Kyōkai. 1937 [1990]. "Bunson kaitaku jirei: Keizai kōsei-son ni okeru Manshū imin bunson keikaku jirei" [Case Studies of the Special Villages for Economic Rehabilitation that Built their Branch Villages in Manchuria]. Reprinted in *Manshū imin kankei shiryō shūsei.* Vol. 7. Tokyo: Fuji Shuppan.
Ochiai, E. 1989. *Kindai kazoku to feminizumu* [The Modern Family and Feminism]. Tokyo: Keisō Shobō.
———. 1994. *21-seiki kazoku e* [Toward the Family of the 21st Century]. Tokyo: Yūhikaku.
Ōkubo, M. 2004. *Aa, waga sokoku yo* [Ah, My Fatherland]. Tokyo: Hassakusha.
Ong, A. 2002. "The Pacific Shuttle: Family, Citizenship, and Capital Circuits." In *The Anthropology of Globalization: A Reader.* Edited by J. X. Inda and R. Rosaldo, 172–97. Oxford: Blackwell.
Orr, J. J. 2001. *The Victim as Hero: Ideologies of Peace and National Identity in Postwar Japan.* Honolulu: University of Hawai'i Press.
Painter, A. 1996. "The Telerepresentation of Women in Japan." In *Reimagining Japanese Women.* Edited by A. E. Imamura, 46–73. Berkeley, CA: University of California Press.
Pharr, S. 1981. *Political Women in Japan: The Search for a Place in Political Life.* Berkeley, CA: University of California Press.
Raymo, J. M. 2003a. "Premarital Living Arrangements and the Transition to First Marriage in Japan." *Journal of Marriage and the Family* 65: 302–15.
———. 2003b. "Educational Attainment and the Transition to First Marriage among Japanese Women." *Demography* 40, No. 1: 83–105.

Saitō, A. 2003. "Ushinawareta farusu o motomete: Kinoshita Keisuke no 'namida no sanbusaku' saikō." In *Eiga no seijigaku*. Edited by M. Hase and H. Makamura, 61–117. Tokyo: Seikyōsha.

Sakai, H. 1995. *Kyōkasho ga kaita kazoku to josei no sengo 50 nen* [The Postwar Family and Women Depicted in Textbooks over 50 Years]. Tokyo: Rōdō Kyōiku Sentā.

Sakamoto, K. 1997. *'Kazoku' imēji no tanjō: Nihon eiga ni miru 'hōmu dorama' no keisei*. Tokyo: Shinyōsha.

Sansom, G. 1963. *A History of Japan, 1615–1867*. Stanford, CA: Stanford University Press.

Sasaki-Uemura, W. 2001. *Organizing the Spontaneous:Citizen Protest in Postwar Japan*. Honolulu: University of Hawai'i Press.

Sassen, S. 1999. *Globalization and Its Discontents: Essays on the New Mobility of People and Money*. New York: New Press.

Satō, T. 1989. *Daiyō kangoku 33 nin no shōgen* [Substitute Police Jails: Testimony of 33 People]. Tokyo: San'ichi Shobō.

Scheper-Hughes, N., and C. Sargent. 1998. *Small Wars: The Cultural Politics of Childhood*. Berkeley, CA: University of California Press.

Schilling, M. 1997. *The Encyclopedia of Japanese Pop Culture*. New York: Weatherhill.

Schodt, F. L. 1997. "Foreword." In *The Wonderful World of Sazae-San*. Vol. 1 by Machiko Hasegawa. 7–9. Tokyo: Kodansha International.

Schudson, M. 1989. "How Culture Works: Perspectives from Media Studies on the Efficacy of Symbols." *Theory and Society* 18, No. 2: 153–80.

Seeley, J. R. 1883. *The Expansion of England: Two Courses of Lectures*. London: Macmillan.

Sekiguchi, Y, S. Fukutō, A. Nagashima, N. Hayakawa, and F. Asano. 2000. *Kazoku to kekkon no rekishi* [The History of Family and Marriage]. Tokyo: Shinwasha.

Shapiro, M. J. 2001. For Moral Ambiguity: National Culture and the Politics of the Family. Minneapolis, MN: University of Minnesota Press.

Shigenobu, F. 2001. *Ringo no ki no shita de anata wo umou to kimeta* [Under an Apple Tree I Decided to Give Birth to You]. Tokyo: Gentōsha.

———. 2005. "Dokubō yori 38: Dono sedai mo rekishi ni taisuru sekinin o ou." [From a Solitary Cell, 38: Every Generation Bears a Responsibility to History]. *Olī-bu no ki* [the Olive Tree]: 8–9.

Shigenobu, M. 2002. *Himitsu: Paresuchina kara sakura no kuni e, haha to watashi no 28 nen* [Secret—From Palestine to the Land of Cherry Blossoms, 28 Years of My Mother and Me]. Tokyo: Kōdansha.

Shimizu, I. 1991. *Manga no rekishi* [The History of Manga]. Tokyo: Iwanami Shoten.

Shindō, K. 1996. *Sazae-san to sono jidai* [Sazae-san and Her Era]. Tokyo: Banseisha.

Shiriagari, K. 2004. *Chikyū bōeike no hitobito* [People of the Earth Defense Family]. Tokyo: Asahi Shinbunsha.

Smith, R. J. 1996. "The Japanese (Confucian) Family: Tradition from the Bottom Up." In *Confucian Traditions in East Asian Modernity: Moral Education and Economic Culture in Japan and the Four Mini-Dragons*. Edited by Wei-ming Tu, 155–74. Cambridge, MA: Harvard University Press.

Smith, R. J. 1989. "Presidential Address: Something Old, Something New: Tradition and Culture in the Study of Japan." *Journal of Asian Studies* 48:715–23.

Sōmushō, ed. 1997. *Kōrei shakai hakusho* [White paper on the aging society]. Tokyo: Sōmushō.

Stacey, J. 1996. *In the Name of the Family: Rethinking Family Values in the Postmodern Age*. Boston, MA: Beacon Press.

Standish, I. 1998. "Akira, Post-modernism and Resistance." In *The Worlds of Japanese Popular Culture*. Edited by D. P. Martinez, 56–74. Cambridge: Cambridge University Press.

Steinhoff, P. G. 1988. "Tenkō and Thought Control." In *The Japanese and the World: Essays on Japanese History and Politics in Honour of Ishida Takeshi*. Edited by G. Bernstein and H. Fukui. London: MacMillan Press.

———. 1991. *Tenkō: Ideology and Societal Integration in Prewar Japan*. New York: Garland Publishing.

———. 1999. "Doing the Defendant's Laundry: Support Groups as Social Movement Organizations in Contemporary Japan." *Japanstudien* 11.

———. 2003. "Notes from the Underground: Doing Fieldwork without a Site." In *Doing Fieldwork in Japan*. Edited by T. C. Bestor, P. G. Steinhoff and V. L. Bestor. Honolulu: University of Hawai'i Press.

———. 2009 forthcoming. "Shifting Boundaries in Japan's Criminal Justice System." In *Decoding Boundaries in Postwar Japan: The Koizumi Administration and Beyond*. Edited by G. D. Hook and H. Takeda. London: Routledge.

Stephens, S. 1995. "Introduction: Children and the Politics of Culture in 'Late Capitalism.' " In *Children and the Politics of Culture*. Edited by S. Stephens, 3–48. Princeton: Princeton University Press.

Takahashi, Y. 1976. "Nihon fashuzumu to 'manshū' nōgyō imin" [The Japanese Fascism and the Agrarian Emigrants to Manchuria]. *Tochi seidoshi-gaku* 71, No. 3: 47–67.

Takazawa, K. 1983. *Furēmu appu: Tsuchida Nisseki pīsukan jiken no shinsō* [Frame-Up: The Truth About the Tsuchida Nisseki Peace Can Incident]. Tokyo: Shinsensha.

———. 1998. *Shukumei: 'Yodogō bōmeishatachi no himitsu kōsaku* [Destiny: The Secret Operations of the 'Yodogō' Exiles]. Tokyo: Shinchōsha.

Takikawa, H. 1973. *Kagekiha kaimetsu sakusen, kōan kisha nikki* [Operation Annihilate the Radicals: A Security Police Reporter's Diary]. Tokyo: San'ichi Shobō.

Talcott, P. 2002. "The Politics of Japan's Long-term Care Insurance System." In *Aging and Social Policy: A German-Japanese Comparison*. Edited by H. Conrad and R. Lützeler, 89–112. Munich: Deutschen Institut für Japanstudien/IUDICIUM Verlag.

Tamanoi, M. A. 2000. "A Road to 'A Redeemed Mankind': The Politics of Memory among the Former Japanese Peasant Settlers in Manchuria." *The South Atlantic Quarterly* 99, No. 1: 163–89.

Teikoku N. 1942 [1990]. *Manshū kaitaku-min sōshutsu chōsa: Nagano-ken Suwa-gun Fujimi-mura* [Survey on the Emigrants to Manchuria: The Case of Fujimi Village in Suwa County, Nagano Prefecture]. Reprinted in *Manshū imin kankei shiryō shūsei*. Vol. 8. Tokyo: Fuji Shuppan.

Tokyo San Bengoshikai Gōdō Daiyō Kangoku Chōsa Iinkai, ed. 1984. *Nureginu: kōshite watashi wa jihaku saserareta* [Unjust Accusations: This is How I Was Forced to Confess]. Tokyo: Seihosha.

Tokyo Sazae-san Gakkai. 1993. *Ijiwaru bāsan no ai* [Granny Ijiwaru's Love]. Tokyo: Mainichi Shinbunsha.

Traphagan, J. W. 2000. *Taming Oblivion: Aging Bodies and the Fear of Senility in Japan*. Albany: State University of New York Press.

———. 2002. "The Liminal Family: Return Migration and Intergenerational Conflict in Japan." *Journal of Anthropological Research* 56:365–85.

———. 2003. "Contesting Coresidence: Women, In-Laws, and Health Care in Rural Japan." In *Demographic Change and the Family in Japan's Aging Society*. Edited by J. W. Traphagan and J. Knight, 203–28. Albany: State University of New York Press.

———. 2004a. *The Practice of Concern: Ritual, Well-Being and Aging in Rural Japan*. Durham, NC: Carolina Academic Press.

———. 2004b. "Curse of the Successor: Filial Piety vs. Marriage Among Rural Japanese." In *Filial Piety: Practice and Discourse in Contemporary East Asia*. Edited by C. Ikels, 198–216. Stanford, CA: Stanford University Press.

Traphagan, J. W., and J. Knight. 2003. *Demographic Change and the Family in Japan's Aging Society*. Albany: State University of New York Press.

Tsuda, T. 2003. *Strangers in the Ethnic Homeland*. New York: Columbia University Press.

Tsuya, N., and L. Bumpass, eds. 2004. *Marriage, Work and Family Life in Comparative Perspective: Japan, South Korea, and the United States*. Honolulu: University of Hawai'i Press.

Ueno, C. 1994. *Kindai kazoku no seiritsu to shūen* [The Rise and Fall of the Modern Family]. Tokyo: Iwanami Shoten.

Uno, K. 1993. "The Death of 'Good Wife, Wise Mother'?" In *Postwar Japan as History*. Edited by A. Gordon, 293–322. Berkeley, CA: University of California Press.

Wada, N. 1993. *Kyū manshū kaitaku-dan no sengo* [The Postwar Conditions of the Former Agrarian Settlers]. Tokyo: Iwanami Shoten.

Wagnleitner, R. 1994. *Coca-Colonization and the Cold War: The Cultural Mission of the United States in Austria after the Second World War*. Chapel Hill, NC: University of North Carolina Press.

White, M. 2002. *Perfectly Japanese: Making Families in an Era of Upheaval*. Berkeley, CA: University of California Press.

———. 1993. *The Material Child: Coming of Age in Japan and America*. Berkeley, CA: University of California Press.

Wu, Y. 2004. *The Care of the Elderly in Japan*. London: Routledge Curzon.

Yamada, M. 2001. *Kazoku to iu risuku* [The Family Risk]. Tokyo: Keisō Shobō.

Yamanaka, K. 1996. "Return Migration of Japanese-Brazilians to Japan: The Nikkeijin as Ethnic Minority and Political Construct." *Diaspora* 5, No. 1: 65–97.

Yampol, H. T. 2005. "Traces of Forgotten Empire: Race and the Identity Of Japanese Colonial "Returnees" from China, 1945–2005." M.A. Thesis, Department of East Asian Languages and Cultures, Indiana University.

Yao, M. 1998a. "Futari no musume ni wa watashi to onaji jinsei o ayumasetakunai!" [I don't Want My Two Daughters to Follow in My Footsteps!]. *Shūkan Gendai* 40:188–92.

———. 1998b. Pyongyang ni iru futari no musume o kaeshite! [Give Me Back My Two Daughters Who Are in Pyongyang!]. *Shūkan Gendai* 40:40–44.

———. 1998c. "Watashi wa Kita-Chōsen de shisō to sei no dorei ni sareta" [I Was Made an Ideology and Sex Slave in North Korea]. Shūkan Gendai. 40:206–10.

———. 2002. *Shazaishimasu* [I Apologize]. Tokyo: Bungei Shunjū.

Yasui, T. 1972. *Hitosuji ni hoshi wa nagarete* [A Lonely Shooting Star]. Tokyo: Taihei Shuppansha.

Yoda, T. 2000. "The Rise and Fall of Maternal Society: Gender, Labor, and Capital in Contemporary Japan." *South Atlantic Quarterly* 99:865–902.

Yoshida, M. 1997. "Contesting Powers: A Cultural Analysis of Water Distribution, Personhood, Gender and Ritual in a Japanese Hot Spring Town." Ph.D. diss. University of Pittsburgh.

Young, L. 1998. *Japan's Total Empire: Manchuria and the Culture of Wartime Imperialism*. Berkeley, CA: University of California Press.

Yuzawa, Y. 2003. *Dēta de yomu kazoku mondai* [Data on Family Issues]. Tokyo: NHK Books.

Zwerman, G. 1994. "Mothering on the Lam: Politics, Gender Conflict and Maternal Thinking in Women Associated with Armed, Clandestine Organizations in the U.S." *Feminist Review* 47:33–56.

Zwerman, G., and P. G. Steinhoff. 2005. "When Activists Ask for Trouble: State-Dissident Interactions and the New Left Cycle of Resistance in the United States and Japan." In *Repression and Mobilization*. Edited by C. Davenport, H. Johnston, and C. Mueller, 85–107. Minneapolis, MN: University of Minnesota Press.

Zwerman, G., P. G. Steinhoff, and D. della Porta. 2000. "Disappearing Social Movements: Clandestinity in the Cycle of New Left Protest in the United States, Japan, Germany and Italy." *Mobilization: An International Quarterly* 5, No. 1: 85–104.

Contributors

AKIKO HASHIMOTO is Associate Professor of Sociology and Asian Studies at the University of Pittsburgh. She was educated at the University of Hamburg, London School of Economics, and Yale University. Before her appointment at the University of Pittsburgh, she was Research Associate at the United Nations University in Tokyo. Her publications include: *The Gift of Generations: Japanese and American Perspectives on Aging and the Social Contract* (Cambridge University Press, 1996), and *Family Support for the Elderly: The International Experience* (Oxford University Press, 1992). She is now at work on projects on citizenship, cultural identity and national memory in postwar Japan, and heroes and villains of Japanese popular culture.

KEIKO I. MCDONALD was Professor of Japanese Cinema and Literature at the University of Pittsburgh. Her major books include: *Cinema East: A Critical Study of Major Japanese Films* (1983); *Mizoguchi* (1984); *Japanese Classical Theater in Films* (1994); *From Book to Screen: Modern Japanese Literature in Films* (2000); and *Reading a Japanese Film: Cinema in Context* (2006). She was working on a book about the filmmaker Hiroshi Shimizu and another on Japanese women directors.

SUSAN J. NAPIER was born and raised in Cambridge, Massachusetts and received her BA, MA, and PhD from Harvard University. She has written four books, including: *Anime from Akira to Howl's Moving Castle* (revised edition 2005), and the forthcoming *From Impressionism to Anime: Japan as Fantasy and Fan Cult in the Western Imagination*. Until 2006 she held the Mitsubishi Heavy Industries Chair of Japanese Studies at the University of Texas at Austin. Currently she is Professor of Japanese at Tufts University.

PATRICIA G. STEINHOFF is Professor of Sociology at the University of Hawaii. She is the author or editor of fourteen books, including three in Japanese, and over eighty articles and book chapters. She is the author of *Shi eno Ideology: Nihon Sekigunha* and the *Japanese Studies in the United States and Canada: Continuities and Opportunities* and has recently edited the third edition of the *Directory of Japan Specialists and Japanese Studies Institutions in the United States and Canada,* and (with Theodore Bestor and Vickey Lyon Bestor) *Doing Fieldwork in Japan.* Her work has appeared in the *Journal of Japanese Studies, Qualitative Sociology,* and *Mobilization.* She is currently writing a book on Japan's invisible civil society.

MARIKO ASANO TAMANOI received her doctorate in anthropology from Northwestern University. She is currently Associate Professor of Anthropology at the University of California, Los Angeles. She is author of *Under the Shadow of Nationalism: Politics and Poetics of Rural Japanese Women,* as well as editor of *Crossed Histories: Manchuria in the Age of Empire.* Her publications also include articles in the *Journal of Asian Studies, Ethnology, Annual Review of Anthropology, Comparative Studies in Society and History,* and *American Ethnologist.* She is preparing a book manuscript titled *Memory Maps: The State and Manchuria in Postwar Japan.*

JOHN W. TRAPHAGAN is Associate Professor of Religious Studies and Anthropology at the University of Texas at Austin. He was educated at the University of Massachusetts Lowell, Yale University, and the University of Pittsburgh. His books include: *Taming Oblivion: Aging Bodies and the Fear of Senility in Japan,* and *The Practice of Concern: Ritual, Well-Being, and Aging in Rural Japan,* as well as several co-edited volumes, the most recent of which is *Wearing Cultural Styles in Japan: Concepts of Tradition and Modernity in Practice* (with Christopher Thompson). His work has also appeared in many scholarly journals, including: *Ethnology,* the *Journal of Anthropological Research, Research on Aging,* and *Alzheimer Disease and Associated Disorders.*

Name Index

Name Index

Subject Index